One Breath at a Time

One Breath at a Time

Navigating the Early Stages of Child Loss

Shannon Hodgetts

First published in 2025 by Dean Publishing
PO Box 119
Mt. Macedon, Victoria, 3441
Australia
deanpublishing.com

Copyright © Shannon Hodgetts

All rights reserved. No part of this publication may be reproduced, stored in a retrieval system or transmitted in any way or by any means, electronic, mechanical, photocopying, recording or otherwise, without the prior written permission of the author and publisher.
Cataloguing-in-Publication Data
National Library of Australia

Title: One Breath at a Time
ISBN: 978-0-646-70880-5
Category: Self-help/bereavement/grief

This book contains discussions and depictions of death, grief, and trauma associated with the loss of a child. Readers may find some of the content triggering and should practise self-care methods to ensure they are comfortable reading the material. If you are experiencing a difficult time and need extra support, remember that help is available.
Lifeline: 13 11 14
Kids Helpline: 1800 55 1800
MensLine: 1300 78 9978
Beyond Blue: 1300 22 4636

The views and opinions expressed in this book are those of the author and do not necessarily reflect the official policy or position of any other agency, publisher, organisation, employer, medical body, psychological body, or company. Assumptions made in the analysis are not reflective of the position of any entity other than the author(s) – and, these views are always subject to change, revision, and rethinking at any time.

The author, publisher or organisations are not to be held responsible for misuse, reuse, recycled and cited and/or uncited copies of content within this book by others.

This book is not intended to replace any professional advice or diagnose or treat any health or mental health issues. It offers the author's experience and insights around a topic that is often considered difficult to talk about. Grief/bereavement is a multi-faceted subject with many differing recommendations and sources. The reader is advised to always seek professional advice and care according to their specific needs and experiences.

Some names and identifying details of others have been changed to protect the privacy of individuals.

Dedication

I dedicate this book to our loving families, our friends who stayed by our side, my soulmate and the love of my life, Dean; and our three precious children: Amalie, with wisdom beyond her years and an inner beauty and strength to carry her into a blessed and fulfilled life; our son Elijah, who brought us the light and joy we so desperately needed; and to Rhys, whose absence our hearts will always yearn for. Thank you for giving us the chance to share our story and help others. We will never stop loving you.

Contents

Introduction: A Journey of Grief and Love 1

Part 1: The Early Days 3
Chapter 1: The Moment Everything Changed 5
Chapter 2: The Fog of Grief 17
Chapter 3: Gasping for Breath – the Physical Toll of Grief 29

Part 2: Navigating Through Grief 45
Chapter 4: The Five Stages of Grief 47
Chapter 5: Coping Mechanisms and Finding Support 55
Chapter 6: The Non-Linear Nature of Grief 71

Part 3: The Search for Solace 77
Chapter 7: Memories and Their Significance 79
Chapter 8: Symbolism and Signs 89
Chapter 9: Healing Through Exploration 99

Part 4: Connection 111
Chapter 10: The Foundations of Family 113
Chapter 11: Support Networks, and the Elephant in the Room 121
Chapter 12: Personal Reflections and Journalling 125

Part 5: Living with Loss   137
Chapter 13: Embracing a New Normal   139
Chapter 14: Rediscovering Purpose   149
Chapter 15: The Negative Thoughts   155

Part 6: Parenting Through Loss   165
Chapter 16: Supporting Siblings   167
Chapter 17: Returning to School, Restoring Normalcy   173
Chapter 18: Grief Regression   185

Part 7: Legacy   193
Chapter 19: Projects and Activities in Rhys's Memory   195
Chapter 20: Giving Back and Helping Others   205
Chapter 21: My 'Why'   211

Part 8: The Journey Continues   225
Chapter 22: Reflections on the Journey   227
Chapter 23: Finding Purpose and Meaning   233
Chapter 24: Moving Forward with Grief   239

Resources for Grieving Parents   246
Acknowledgements   255
About the Author   257

Every person must have permission and space to grieve the loss of their child in his or her way, without judgement.

Introduction

A Journey of Grief and Love

Losing a child, regardless of the circumstances or age, is a devastating and heartbreaking experience. Grief, disbelief, and sorrow can become overwhelming in the days, weeks, and years that follow. Navigating this process is incredibly difficult. By sharing our story – a story of courage, pain, hope, and love – I hope to help others identify the challenges, heartbreak and complexities of living life following the death of a child.

This book contains excerpts from my journal to Rhys, written over 3 years, beginning the day he died. Writing to Rhys was such a critical aspect of my journey and it forms part of the person I am today. I carry Rhys in my heart and he remains with me every step of the way.

Part 1

The Early Days

Chapter 1

The Moment Everything Changed

It was Book Week 2016, and the excitement was in full force in our house. Five-year-old Ammi was adamant to dress as a Tasmanian devil this year. During our recent trip to the local zoo, she instantly became affectionate for the cuddly yet ferocious native creature. With the book and stuffed toy already in our possession, the only missing element was the costume. Fortunately, Dean, a skilled builder by trade, has a natural talent for creativity. He has always been the go-to parent for designing and constructing the kids' birthday cakes, crafting laser-cut name signs for bedroom shelves, and building life-sized custom versions of board games like KerPlunk. Whenever a project required a sketch and a level, Dean would leverage his carpentry skills to deliver outstanding results.

Ammi wearing her Book Week Tassie devil costume.

Overcoming last-minute challenges is a forte in the Hodgetts household. After a long day running our construction business, Dean fetched the dusty sewing machine from the archives, a bottle of red from the kitchen, and got to work. With a concept plan drawn to a technical scale, he commenced his most important project of the day, creating a fluffy black vest with a signature white chest and a long fluffy tail for Ammi to wear with pride in 2 days' time at the Book Week parade.

It was common for Rhys to pick up viral illnesses at his beloved day care. A room full of busy 2-year-olds with no concept of personal space made for endless snotty noses and a bunch of colourful yet mild infections we had never heard of prior to having

THE EARLY DAYS

children! Rhys was mildly unwell, so we called the home doctor just to check that he was okay. As was typical, by the time the doctor arrived, Rhys had improved, and he answered the door to the doctor in his singlet and nappy, eating an apple. The GP confirmed, as we had suspected, a viral infection. She instructed us to control his temperature with Panadol, let him get lots of rest, and see our usual GP if he got any worse. Pretty standard for our Rhys.

When Rhys was sick, he would always run a temperature. He had previously suffered from a handful of febrile convulsions – fever-related seizures that are caused by a sudden change in a child's temperature. They were scary to witness. Even though we were reassured that they weren't dangerous, we always called an ambulance.

With dinner, dishes, bath, and nudie run complete, Ammi and Rhys headed off to bed, Rhys with a dose of Panadol on board. A common place for Dean and I to sit was at our kitchen bench. We'd chat about our days while preparing dinner or sewing projects. This night, we enjoyed each other's company, having a quiet chat while the kids drifted off to sleep. As Rhys settled each night, his 2-year-old demands were high. Never was there a night when he didn't yell out at the top of his lungs, "Maaaa" or, "Daaaa" just to sneak in one final demand for the day. "Water," "Eee Eee," "Me up?" "Dummy." The list was endless and obviously typical of your average busy 2-year-old boy.

This night was different. As we chatted quietly in the kitchen of our little home, Rhys called out in a soft, harmonic voice, "Mu-mmy."

Dean and I looked at each other confused and cracked a little laugh, saying, "What's with that?"

I headed down to Rhys's bedroom. When I entered, he was standing up on his bed, arms stretched out, with a huge, beautiful smile on his face. A feeling of warmth consumed my body as I mirrored his smile back at him.

"Night night, Mummy," he said, as we gave each other the biggest cuddle.

"Night night, bubba, sweet dreams, my boy," I said, and Rhys snuggled back into his racing car bed, his blanket and Eee Eee, his toy monkey, tucked under his chin.

I returned to Dean, who was working on Ammi's costume, in the kitchen and made a comment about how strange that was and how soft and gentle our feisty red-headed boy just behaved. Before I finished my sentence, we heard a sweet chant, "Da-ddy." We smiled at each other as Dean put down the fluffy costume and headed down to Rhys's bedroom. He was greeted in the same way. Rhys standing up, arms out wide, a beaming smile on his face. "Night night, Daddy."

Dean hugged Rhys and replied, "Night, mate. Off to sleep now, okay?"

Rhys nodded. "Yes, Daddy," he replied and lay down for Dean to tuck him in.

Rhys never woke up.

The Moment of Loss

The next morning, it was a slow start after a late night of costume-making. Dean and Ammi were in the bathroom, getting ready for work and school. As I sat on the edge of our bed, I remember thinking it was strange that Rhys was sleeping through all the chatter in the bathroom, which was right next to his bedroom.

I got up and bumped into Dean outside Rhys's door. We both went in to find Rhys looking like he was still asleep, but I had a gut feeling something wasn't right. Dean walked over to Rhys, turned around, pressed his phone into my chest, and forced me out the door. He gently closed Rhys's door and walked me into our bedroom, right beside Rhys's room. With his hand still on his phone and one hand on my shoulder, he made eye contact and calmly but firmly said, "You need to call an ambulance."

Initial Reactions and Shock

The next few moments I cannot put into words. Dean put Ammi in her bedroom and went back in with Rhys. I was in our room with 000 on speakerphone while my whole life flashed before my eyes. I couldn't speak. Dean was walking between the three bedrooms. When he came back into our room, he took the phone and confirmed to the operator that there was nothing that could be done.

It took 6 minutes for the ambulance to arrive. So many flashes from that day, like photographs in dusty frames, hanging on a wall in a dark, empty room. Arrivals. The police, more ambulances, more police. The coroner. Cameras, people talking quietly. Solemn expressions. Deathly calm filling our house. The sewing machine still on the kitchen table. Family arriving. Standing up, sitting down. Our darling Ammi. Employees, who are like family, turning up to start work for the day. The first responding constables – I will never forget how young they both were, not long out of the academy. Questions, trying to recall information, such as our phone numbers, our dates of birth. Being paralysed by shock. Comfort from our family, from responders, police ringing Ammi's school to say she wouldn't be in that day. The overwhelming sense of shock and calm is what I remember most.

A couple of hours passed, and the paramedics asked how we wanted Rhys to be moved to the ambulance. Dean was adamant that he would carry Rhys outside. We went to Rhys's room, where we were supported to carry Rhys in his dad's arms. Emergency services formed a guard of honour from our front door to the ambulance. We will never forget the way we were supported that day by the responders. Absolute heroes.

THE EARLY DAYS

22/8/16

Goodnight sweet baby. Mummy and Daddy love you with all our hearts. Eee Eee is sleeping in our bed tonight. Please watch over us all including Amalie.

That night and the next few days are a blur. Our siblings from Melbourne and family and friends from interstate and abroad arrived and remained by our sides. Ammi was wrapped in love and kept busy while Dean and I prepared a funeral for our son, something a parent should never, ever have to do.

26/8/16

We have been to spend time with you today and yesterday. You handed over every ounce of strength you had, and Mummy and Daddy have shared it between us. You make us feel so privileged to have had you in our lives. You lived 20 years in 2 and a half. We should have known you were sent to us to make us super strong. We are so at peace seeing you sleeping. Everything is set to go for Tuesday. We've got some lovely surprises there for you. Goodnight my angel xxxxxx

I was scared to see Rhys at the funeral home. I remember feeling sick to my stomach as we approached the room but once I was there with Dean, a massive weight was lifted from my shoulders.

Our celebrant gently encouraged us to see it as a celebration of Rhys's life as opposed to a child's funeral. Once we chose to do this, it made planning bearable.

I felt so close to Rhys; he was just beautiful. Something surreal happened that day. We both felt an overwhelming surge of strength consume us. The strength that would see us keep fighting throughout the years was gifted to us that day.

27/8/16
It has been sunny every day since you went to heaven. Get us through another day bubba xx

We are so tired tonight my darling. We have been watching videos of you having so much fun with Mummy, Daddy and Ammi. You are so, so funny, and clever. Going to bed now bunny, I need rest xxx

29/8/16
Tomorrow is your celebration bubba. You make Mummy and Daddy very proud Rhys. Promise me you will get us through tomorrow. We will see you in the morning to say goodbye to your body. You live in our hearts, so you are always with us. It is one step closer to bringing you home my darling. Eee Eee is waiting to see you and tiger dummy. Goodnight my angel xxxxxxxxx

30/8/16 (Funeral)

Today is the day to celebrate you, Rhys. This is it. Stay close to Mummy, Daddy, and Ammi, and pull us through this. We love you xxx

Planning a funeral for your son is nothing short of completely earth-shattering.

We started collecting photos, videos, and songs. It kept us busy and focused, with an end goal in sight. It was a beautiful celebration of Rhys. I didn't speak on the day, and sometimes I regret that choice, but we did the best we could, and I don't beat myself up over it.

We had a house full of flowers, donated from all over the country. It was a remarkable sight by which we were truly humbled. We had no idea what to do with the flowers, as we didn't want to throw them out. Someone suggested we take them to the funeral home, and every single flower we received went with Rhys to be cremated with him. Another gesture that brings us comfort, knowing all the love went with him to protect him.

It's over bubba. Thank you for getting us through. We love you so much. There were so many people there today. We played videos of you, we couldn't help but smile. We had Mr. Bean playing before the service. It was truly an amazing celebration of your life. It makes me so proud of you. Tonight we had family and our special people over after the service. Uncle Joel sang some songs and we all talked, cried, and laughed together. I'm so tired now, it's been the hardest day of our lives Rhys. Love you bubba xxx

31/8/16
I miss Mummy cuddles. I don't know how I feel Rhys. I feel calm, numb, sad, happy and irritated. I feel you with me every second of the day. Just one more kiss and cuddle. It is very quiet without you. There were a lot of people at your funeral. We are surrounded by so much love but why do I feel so alone? They will return to their everyday lives, and we are left here without you.

I'm going to make a promise to you. Daddy, Ammi, and I will cherish every single moment of our lives, thanks to you, my precious boy. Sweet dreams Mr Mouse. xxx

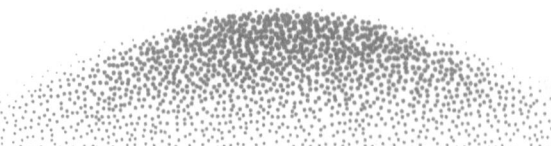

A Breath of Wisdom

During the initial stages of
shock and grief, support from
family and friends is vital.

If you can't bring yourself to perform
a certain task, such as speaking at
your child's funeral, don't beat yourself
up over it. Just do the best you can.

Through loss, we can gain a level of
strength we never thought possible.

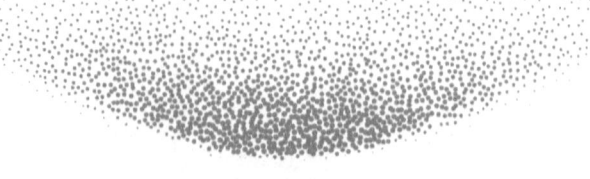

Chapter 2

The Fog of Grief

The early days following the loss of a child are marked by a profound sense of shock and disbelief beyond explanation. It's a period where the world seems to stand still, and the weight of your loss feels unbearable. This chapter delves into the initial phase of grief, often called the 'grief fog', where emotions are raw and the reality of the loss is just beginning to sink in.

The Initial Shock

The moment you learn of your child's passing, your life changes irrevocably. This initial shock is overwhelming, and your mind struggles to comprehend the magnitude of the loss. In these first days, you might find yourself in a state of numbness, where everything feels surreal. This numbness is a natural protective mechanism that shields you from the full impact of your grief.

For me, the news of Rhys's death was a moment frozen in time. I remember the world blurring around me, sounds becoming distant, and a cold numbness spreading through my body. It felt as though I was an observer in my own life, detached and disconnected from reality.

Brain Fog

Early days, weeks, and months of child loss are a confusing and lonely place. It's a hollow hole in a misty abyss. Early days are surreal, and it's hard to focus and exist. It's a time when you generally experience brain fog.

My experience involved learning cognitive skills again. How to pack the dishwasher, how to cook. It's a distressing time, and it can last weeks, months, or years. It felt like a type of protection, a coping mechanism. During this time, I slept when I could and just went through the motions. I remember telling myself, *The day ahead will be okay if I can just get out of bed and open the blinds.* If I did that, I was going to be okay.

During this time, I spent a lot of my days in Ammi's prep classroom. Pinning artwork to walls, helping the children with simple tasks. I was lost and didn't know what I was supposed to be doing. Ammi's teacher gave me space to feel safe and less alone. In silence, in conversation, in song, in reading. I'm so grateful for the actions of others during that time.

One of my best friends joined the gym with me, and we went a few days a week. The gym released a lot of emotional build up, and the endless banter and shit-stirring gave my mind a rest! It wasn't anything huge, but I look back now and see the positive impact it made.

6/9/16

Yesterday was a hard day Daddy and I wish to forget it, but we keep moving forward for you and Ammi. Today was a bit better. Baby steps.

I was so pleased to pick up my locket today. It is so beautiful, and your body is now close to my heart, where your soul lives bubba.

There is such a hole left in our lives, home, daily routine. I can't wait to see you and hold you again one day in heaven, my precious baby boy. It would be so easy to let go of everything and just give up but we can't. We keep putting one foot in front of the other and keep living our lives for you and Ammi. It's our only option.

I clearly remember the day we collected Rhys's ashes from the funeral home. We didn't want Rhys to be in the cemetery. A plaque was to be installed at his day care, and Ammi's school also offered to install a plaque. We thought three was a bit much; plus we wanted his ashes at home with us. Dean suggested that when I die, Rhys's ashes will come with me. These conversations seem absurd now, but at the time it was practical and made sense.

7/9/16

We got to bring your ashes home today darling. We have you back in your bedroom where you belong, at home, safe with Mummy, Daddy and Ammi. Thanks for sending us the most amazing sign as we approached the front door, Dad holding your ashes. Daddy said 'look up to the sky'. There was the brightest star we have ever seen, shining brightly on us, not another star was to be seen in the sky. We knew it was you, telling us you were home now and that we will be ok. Thank you Rhysy. Sleep tight Mr Mouse. Please stay with me, I need you to carry me, my strong little man xxxx

The Grief Fog

The concept of the 'grief fog' describes the mental and emotional haze that engulfs you in the early days, weeks, and months of grief. This fog can affect your ability to think clearly, make decisions, and perform even the simplest tasks. You may feel like you're moving through a dreamlike state, where nothing seems real or tangible.

During this time, everyday activities like eating, sleeping, and communicating with others become challenging. You might forget to eat or lose your appetite altogether. Sleep can be elusive, with your mind racing through a tumult of thoughts and emotions. Conversations can feel draining, and you may find it difficult to articulate your feelings or even engage in basic interactions.

> *8/9/16*
>
> *I can't keep track of what day it is. Nanna came for tea tonight. She played Barbies with Ammi. I'm worried about how Ammi is going. She misses you Rhys, we miss you. My heart aches, it feels like I have something physically wrong with my heart. I just want to cuddle you. I'd do anything for one cuddle or just to touch your hand. I don't know how I'm going to live without you xx*

Coping with the Fog

Navigating through the grief fog requires patience and self-compassion. Here are some strategies that helped me during this overwhelming time:

- **Take it one day at a time.** Focus on getting through one day, or even one moment, at a time.

- **Set small, manageable goals.** Allow yourself to move slowly. By this, I mean set goals such as 'eat something' or 'take a shower'.

- **Accept help from others.** Allow friends and family to assist with daily tasks. Whether it's preparing meals, helping with household chores, or simply being there for you, accepting help can provide some relief. Don't hesitate to rest while people are in your home helping. They'll be comforted by the fact that you're able to rest due to their assistance.

- **Create a routine.** Establishing a simple routine can bring a sense of structure to your day. Even small rituals, like making a cup of tea or taking a short walk, can provide a semblance of normalcy.

- **Express your emotions.** Cry when you need to, scream if you must, and write down your thoughts and feelings. Expressing your emotions can be a crucial outlet for your grief. Listen to music or look at photos if you feel your sadness is 'stuck'.

- **Seek professional support.** Grief counsellors and therapists can offer a safe space to explore your emotions and provide strategies to cope with the intense feelings of loss. Personally, I struggled with this, but it may help others.

The Role of Shock and Numbness

While the numbness of the grief fog can be disorienting, it also serves an essential purpose. This initial shock acts as a buffer, allowing you to process the loss gradually.

As the shock begins to wear off, you may experience waves of intense emotions. These can be frightening and overwhelming, but they're a natural part of the grieving process. Allow yourself to ride these waves, knowing that it's okay to feel whatever emotions arise.

It's important to recognise that feeling numb doesn't mean you're not grieving. Instead, it's your mind's way of protecting you from taking the full brunt of your sorrow all at once.

Finding Moments of Clarity

Even in the midst of the grief fog, there will be brief moments of clarity. These moments might come unexpectedly – a memory that brings a smile, a conversation that feels meaningful, or a quiet moment of reflection. Cherish these moments, as they can provide glimpses of hope and a reminder that healing, although slow, is possible.

One such moment for me was finding a photograph of Rhys tucked away in a drawer. Seeing his smiling face, even for a brief moment, brought a mix of pain and comfort. It was a reminder of the love and joy he brought into my life, and it gave me a fleeting sense of connection amid the overwhelming grief. I also bought a necklace and have his ashes in the pendant so he's always with me, close to my heart.

Moving Forward Through the Fog

As time passes, the grief fog will gradually begin to lift. The numbness will fade, and the reality of your loss will become more tangible. This transition can be both a relief and a new source of pain. While the fog can dull the sharp edges of your grief, its lifting forces you to confront the full weight of your sorrow. It's important to be gentle with yourself during this transition.

The early days of grief and the accompanying grief fog are some of the most challenging times you will face. The shock and numbness serve as initial protections, giving you the space to begin processing your loss. By taking small steps, accepting help, and expressing your emotions, you can navigate through this fog. Remember, it's a gradual journey, and finding moments of clarity and support can provide the strength needed to move forward. Through it all, know that you're not alone and that your journey through grief, though painful, is a testament to the profound love you have for your child.

Shannon wearing the pendant that contains Rhys's ashes.

THE EARLY DAYS

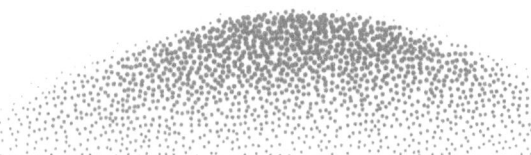

A Breath of Wisdom

When the reality of loss is still stinking in, we can experience 'grief fog'.

Focus on taking it one day, one moment at a time.

Allow yourself to ride the waves of your emotions – they're a natural part of the grieving process.

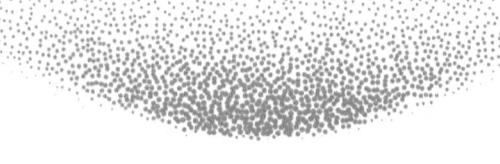

Chapter 3

Gasping for Breath – the Physical Toll of Grief

The loss of a child is an indescribable anguish that permeates every aspect of a parent's existence. It's not just an emotional or psychological battle, but a physical one as well. Many grieving parents describe feeling as though they're gasping for breath, suffocating under the weight of their sorrow. This chapter explores the profound physical effects of grief, focusing on the sensation of struggling to breathe and the broader physiological impacts that accompany such an immense loss.

The Breathlessness of Grief

In the wake of losing Rhys, I often felt as if the air had been sucked out of the room. There were moments when the weight of my grief was so overwhelming that it felt like I couldn't draw a full breath. This sensation is common among bereaved parents and can manifest in various ways, such as tightness in the chest, shortness of breath, and a feeling of suffocation.

Grief can trigger a fight-or-flight response in the body, releasing stress hormones like cortisol and adrenaline. This physiological reaction, while helpful in short-term emergencies, can become detrimental when sustained over long periods, as is often the case with profound grief. The constant state of heightened alert can lead to chronic physical symptoms, including the feeling of being unable to breathe, tension, anxiety, and exhaustion.

The Physical Manifestations of Grief

Grief is not solely an emotional experience. It manifests in the body in several tangible ways, impacting physical health and wellbeing. Here are some common physical symptoms experienced by grieving parents:

- **Chest pain and tightness.** The sensation of a heavy weight pressing down on the chest is common. This pain can be acute and alarming, often mimicking the symptoms of a heart attack.

- **Shortness of breath.** Many parents report struggling to breathe deeply or feeling as though they're constantly out of breath. This can be a direct result of anxiety and stress caused by grief.

- **Fatigue and exhaustion.** Grief drains your energy, leading to persistent tiredness and physical exhaustion. Simple tasks can become monumental challenges.

- **Sleep disturbances.** Insomnia, restless sleep, and nightmares are common. The mind's inability to shut off can lead to nights spent tossing and turning, further depleting your physical reserves.

- **Muscle tension and aches.** The body often holds stress in the muscles, leading to chronic pain, stiffness, and tension, particularly in the neck, shoulders, and back.

- **Headaches and migraines.** Persistent headaches and migraines can occur, driven by the constant stress and emotional strain of grief.

- **Appetite changes.** Some people lose their appetite entirely, while others may turn to food for comfort, leading to significant weight loss or gain.

The Intersection of Mind and Body

The connection between emotional pain and physical symptoms is well-documented. Grief can cause the nervous system to become dysregulated, leading to symptoms that mimic physical illness. For instance, the sensation of breathlessness may stem from hyperventilation or panic attacks, which are common responses to intense stress and anxiety.

Recognising these symptoms as a natural part of the grieving process is crucial. Understanding that your body is reacting to your emotional turmoil can help alleviate some of the fear and confusion these physical symptoms cause.

Coping with the Physical Effects of Grief

Keeping it basic and taking a holistic approach worked best for me. The following might help a grieving parent:

- **Breathing exercises.** Gentle deep breaths in and out can help regulate the nervous system and alleviate the sensation of breathlessness.

- **Physical activity.** Gentle movement can help release built-up tension and improve overall wellbeing.

- **Hydration and nutrition.** I'll be honest – this wasn't at the top of my list after losing Rhys, but I understand (as most people do) the importance of maintaining a healthy diet and staying hydrated. I also know that grief can lead to neglecting self-care, and it's nice to be reminded that proper nutrition and hydration, without external pressures, are crucial to physical health.

- **Rest and relaxation.** Prioritise rest and allow yourself to take breaks when needed.

- **Professional support.** Consider seeking help from healthcare professionals when you're ready. It doesn't work for everyone, but therapists who specialise in grief, and physicians who can address physical symptoms, may be able to assist. Medication or therapeutic interventions may be necessary for managing severe anxiety or depression. Dean and I explored other therapies, and the stand-out, discussed further in chapter five, is EFT (emotional freedom technique) therapy, which I still use regularly.

- **Expressing emotions.** Finding healthy outlets for your emotions can prevent them from manifesting physically. Writing, talking with supportive friends or family, music, and engaging in creative activities can help you process your grief.

The physical toll of grief is a testament to the profound impact that the loss of a child has on a parent.

The Importance of Self-Compassion

Living with the physical effects of grief requires a great deal of self-compassion. It's important to recognise that these symptoms are a natural response to an unnatural loss. Be gentle with yourself and give yourself permission to feel and heal at your own pace.

Remember, there's no timeline for grief, and it's okay to seek help and lean on others during this time. The sensation of gasping for breath may lessen over time, but it's crucial to address your physical and emotional needs proactively.

The feeling of being unable to breathe, the chronic fatigue, and the myriad of other physical symptoms are all part of the body's response to immense sorrow. By acknowledging these symptoms and taking steps to care for your physical and emotional health, you can begin to navigate the challenging journey of living with loss. Remember, healing is a gradual process, and it's okay to seek support and take it one breath at a time.

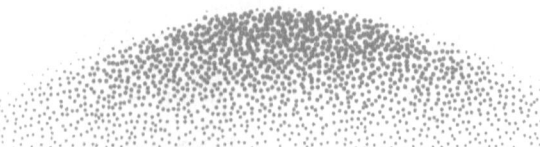

A Breath of Wisdom

Grief can manifest as physical symptoms, such as shortness of breath and exhaustion.

Certain practices, such as breathing exercises and physical activity, can help alleviate the physical symptoms of grief.

Be gentle with yourself and allow yourself to heal at your own pace.

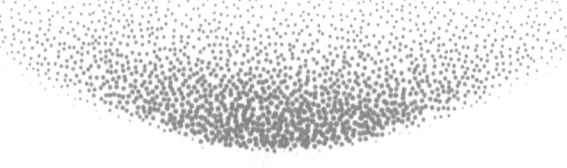

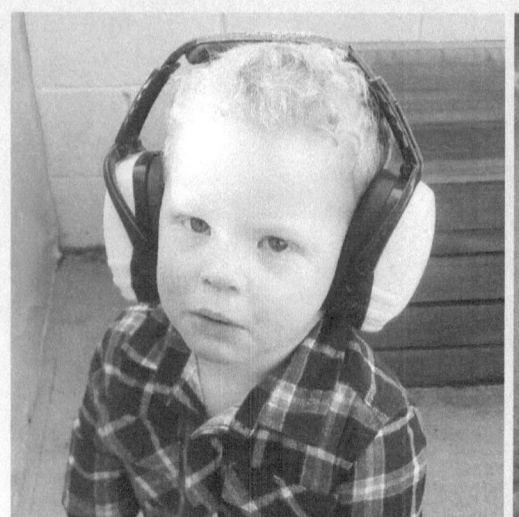

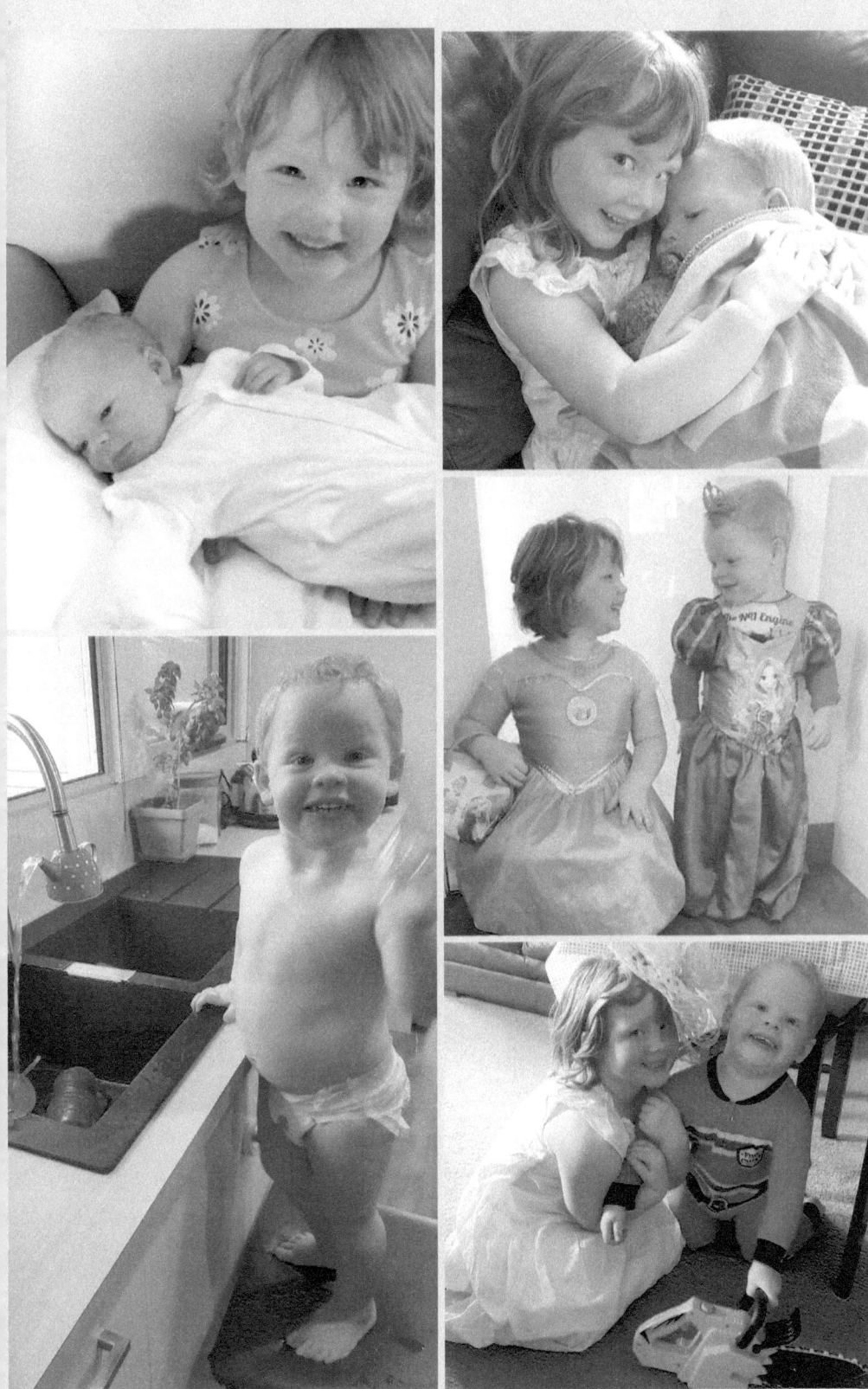

Part 2

Navigating Through Grief

Chapter 4
The Five Stages of Grief

The five stages of grief – denial, bargaining, depression, anger, and acceptance – are like old friends to me now. I float between them. Their force was much stronger in the early days, and some stages are less familiar now.

Personal Reflections on Denial

I'll never forget the pain and despair of denial. Denial hit me like a truck. It was powerful, consuming, and overwhelming. It hit over and over again, several times a day. I remember when I refused to accept the reality of Rhys's death. It was as if my heart and mind had put up a barrier to protect me from the unbearable truth. I kept repeating to myself that it was just a nightmare and each night I went to bed, I begged to wake up and have it all be over.

The 'What Ifs' and 'If Onlys'

Bargaining was my desperate attempt to make sense of the senseless. I replayed events in my mind, thinking of all the 'what ifs' and 'if onlys'. These moments consumed my thoughts and made basic tasks impossible. I couldn't think logically because thoughts overtook my mind. All those moments when I felt as though I'd failed as a parent came to the fore, one by one, torturing me and blaming me for Rhys's death. Although I confided this information to some people and had their support, nothing anyone said brought me peace. I knew it was myself I had to confront, and it took me years to accept that I had no control over Rhys's death.

This stage is less prominent now, but there are still times when my mind drifts back to the countless scenarios I wished could have been different. I now have the tools to stop this thought pattern, and I focus on what a wonderful mother I am, recalling specific examples as evidence to remind myself.

The Deep Sadness of Loss

Losing a child is, in my opinion and that of many others, the most incomprehensible experience a human being can face. The depth is so catastrophic. The most common phrase I've heard from people when discussing Rhys's death is, "I can't even imagine what that's like." It's the truth. No one can mentally and emotionally put themselves in the shoes of a parent who has lost a child, and that's okay!

In the early days, I don't think I had depression. While I had previously been depressed, I couldn't label the sensation I was experiencing as depression. It was a numbness of the soul, body, and mind, and it settled in like a heavy fog, enveloping my days in sorrow and emptiness. I would come up for air when 'interacting' with others. I remember it being like I was daydreaming; then someone would click their fingers to wake me up. The weight of losing Rhys felt too heavy to bear, and there were times when it seemed like the sadness would never lift.

Dealing with Anger in Daily Life

Anger still presents itself, sometimes unexpectedly. It flares up in moments of frustration and helplessness, targeting the unfairness of the situation and the loss of Rhys. This anger can be directed at anything and anyone, from the circumstances of Rhys's death to the world around me. It's a raw and intense emotion, a reminder of the deep love and profound loss I feel. It's not as frequent now, but it certainly was a very lonely feeling in the early days.

I knew bottling it up wouldn't end well. When the anger became unbearable, I'd turn to alcohol to mask my emotions and get some reprieve. It's what I needed at the time, but it never did me any favours.

Acceptance and Understanding

Acceptance remains a controversial topic among bereaved parents. While I accept that Rhys has died, I refuse to accept why it was him and why it happened to us. Acceptance, in this context, doesn't mean being okay with the loss or understanding it fully. Instead, it means recognising the reality of the situation. For me, it's an ongoing process, one that I navigate daily, acknowledging the loss while continuing to live and love. This doesn't mean I don't feel guilty for still being alive. Rhys only lived for 2 years, and I'm in my 40s. It may sound cliché, but I'll use this opportunity to create a legacy to help others in his honour.

There were no answers to my questions; it was just important that I had the space to vent and be angry at the world.

Regardless of a bereaved parent's experience, it's crucial to honour each stage and not force a change in stages. Grief isn't linear; it's a personal journey that looks different for everyone. These stages serve as a framework, but each individual's experience will vary. It's important to let yourself feel each emotion, process the pain, and find your way through the darkness. Appreciate those 'click of the fingers' moments that bring you out into the light, even if only briefly. Upon reflection, these are the beacons that lead me out of the dark.

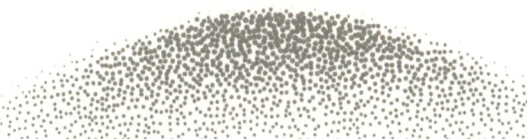

A Breath of Wisdom

While no one can mentally and emotionally put themselves in the shoes of someone who has lost a child, they can still offer support.

Strong emotions, such as anger, are a reminder of the deep love and loss you feel.

Acceptance isn't about being okay with your loss but instead about accepting the reality of the situation.

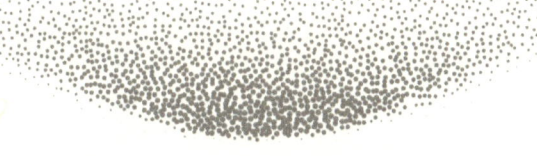

Chapter 5
Coping Mechanisms and Finding Support

Grieving the loss of a child is a journey that no parent is ever truly prepared for. The pain and sorrow can feel insurmountable, but finding effective coping mechanisms and support systems is crucial in navigating this heartbreaking path. In this chapter, I will share some of the strategies that have helped me, as well as insights from other bereaved parents, to offer a diverse range of tools for managing grief.

Before diving into specific coping mechanisms, it's important to understand that grief is highly individual. There's no right or wrong way to grieve, and the process can vary greatly from one person to another. What works for one parent might not work for another, and that's okay. The key is to find what brings you comfort and helps you process your emotions.

One of the first steps in coping with grief is allowing yourself to feel. It can be tempting to suppress your emotions to avoid the pain, but acknowledging and experiencing these feelings is essential for healing. Cry when you need to, express your anger, and permit yourself to feel sadness. Bottling up emotions can lead to greater suffering over time.

Journalling and Writing

For me, writing has been a lifeline. Keeping a journal where I could pour out my thoughts and feelings provided a safe space to process my grief. I began writing letters to Rhys the day he died, and continued for 3 years. These letters helped me articulate my pain, my memories, and my hopes. Looking back, these journals document my journey through grief and serve as a reminder of how far I've come.

I've included content from my journal to Rhys throughout this book in an attempt to show supporting family and friends of bereaved parents what was going through my mind in the early days. This content is raw and captures the desperation I felt at the time.

Self-Care

The waves of grief were a significant force in earlier days. The waves hit you like a freight train. As soon as you think you've ridden one out, the next one scoops you up, the force pulling you down as you gasp for air. It's a cruel process and although it subsides over time, I still ride these waves. They're just easier to manage now. Back then, they were crippling.

I didn't actively think to myself that self-care was important. I never felt in control of my self-care. Many people suggested self-care, but I didn't think, *Okay, that's what I need to do.* I was barely functioning, let alone looking for ways to look after myself. I guess the layers were peeled right back and I found a subconscious way to cope. For me, it was journalling, seeing people for a chat when I felt up to it, sleeping, and music. For Dean, it was working in the shed, working on the boat, and music. To rest and slow things right down, both of us needed time on our own, with each other, with Ammi, with family, and with close friends.

I found it important to take time to acknowledge and honour my emotions, but it certainly didn't come naturally. It was something I struggled with. Though it may be tempting to hide from sadness or push away your grief, allow yourself to grieve, but in whatever way is most comforting for you. A psychologist taught me how to recognise my emotions as they came and to sit with them. This laid the foundation for coping, and I still use these skills when I'm in a bad space.

11/9/16

I wasn't there for you when you died Rhys. I just want to say sorry. I feel like I've abandoned you, how lonely you must be without your Mummy. You needed me constantly when you were here. How can that nurturing just stop? I'm so utterly lost without you.

Not even 1 month after Rhys died, I could feel his spiritual presence slipping away from me, and it was scary. His physical body was gone, I knew that, but in a desperate attempt while deep in the denial stage of grief, I relied on him to keep us strong. It was an internal survival tactic, as I can see now. It was all we had, apart from Ammi, that was keeping us alive.

12/9/16

Busy day today bub. Very tired now. We had a big family cuddle tonight. I felt you were there. We love you baby. It's just not the same without you here. I went to visit daycare again today. They were having morning tea. It was very quiet in there. I saw your beautiful painting you did of the Olympic rings. You are such a clever boy. Mummy is so very proud of you. Stay with us Rhys xxx

15/9/16

Life is so different without you. We are still getting by day by day. We miss you. I've been dreaming about you Rhys, is that you visiting me? It's beautiful to hold you in my dreams. Goodnight sweet boy xxx

Physical Activity

Engaging in physical activity can be a powerful way to cope with grief. Exercise releases endorphins, which can help improve your mood and reduce stress. Whether it's going for a walk, practising yoga, or even just stretching, incorporating movement into your daily routine can provide a much-needed outlet for your emotions.

Creative Expression

Creative activities such as painting, drawing, or playing music can also be therapeutic. These forms of expression allow you to channel your grief into something tangible and beautiful. Many parents find solace in creating art that honours their child's memory, turning their pain into a tribute of love and remembrance.

20/9/16

It hasn't been a good couple of days my darling. Mummy feels sad because you are in heaven, and I miss you so much. It feels like a burning in my chest and my throat. It hurts a lot. I'm hoping tomorrow will be a better day. I must keep getting up and opening the bedroom blind. It means I'm going to be ok for another day. I will make you proud Rhys. I will give it my everything, every day of my life until we can have mummy cuddles again. I hope you are enjoying playing with your little angel friends. Please stay with us baby. We can't do this alone xxx

Seeking Professional Help

There's no shame in seeking professional help. Therapists and counsellors who specialise in grief can offer invaluable support. They can provide you with coping strategies, help you navigate complex emotions, and offer a non-judgemental space to talk about your loss. Group therapy can also be beneficial, as it connects you with others who understand what you're going through.

Support Groups

Connecting with other bereaved parents can be incredibly comforting. Support groups, whether in-person or online, offer a sense of community and understanding that's difficult to find elsewhere. Sharing your story and hearing others' experiences can validate your feelings and provide new perspectives on coping with grief. I found solace in a private Facebook group called Bittersweet Parents, which is managed by Lisa Bird.

Bittersweet Parents Facebook group:
www.facebook.com/groups/bittersweetparents/

Spiritual and Religious Support

For many, spirituality and religion offer comfort and hope during times of immense sorrow. Engaging in prayer, meditation, or other spiritual practices can provide a sense of peace and connection to something greater than yourself. Many faith communities also offer support groups and counselling services for those dealing with loss.

While I don't practise religion myself, I think of myself as a spiritual person, and signs from Rhys following his death were definitely something that kept me going. An example of this – a month after Rhys died, we travelled to Melbourne where my brother, his wife, and their children live. At the time, their son was 6 years old, and their twin girls had just turned 3. We were in their living room, and the girls were at the dining table drawing…

24/9/16

Something funny happened tonight Rhysy. Were you whispering in your cousin's ear because she drew a picture of a 'little boy who was talking to her and was very funny' and she wrote OLPOP backwards. Remember that's how you said lollipop? It certainly took us all by surprise!

Drawing of the 'little boy' by Rhys's cousin.

Everyone has been talking about Olpops. We had a big basket of them at your funeral, you would have loved it. Anyway, keep being cheeky my darling and keep sending us signs. They keep me going xxxx

Leaning on Loved Ones

Don't hesitate to lean on your family and friends for support. It can be difficult to ask for help, but those who care about you want to be there for you. Let them know what you need, whether it's someone to listen, help with daily tasks, or just a comforting presence.

My brother and I video called each other every week. We made sure it was in our calendars so it happened and became a ritual. Sometimes we chatted; sometimes we just sat and cried. It was the best we could do when living so far away from each other.

I'd hear from my sisters-in-law via Messenger on a regular basis, almost daily.

Messenger was a great way of communicating. It allowed me space to respond when I was available but also when I was feeling up for a chat. I'd constantly have messages waiting for me in my inbox, and it made me feel supported and less alone.

Our beautiful best friends arranged for Dean, Amalie, and I to stay at their family shack for a weekend. Keys were dropped to

Surrounding yourself with
a supportive network can
make a significant difference
in your healing process.

us, and I remember the weekend as a beautiful moment in time. These kind gestures go a long way in helping with healing and creating new memories.

Creating Memorials and Rituals

Creating a memorial or engaging in rituals can help you honour your child's memory. Planting a tree, dedicating a bench, or even having a special piece of jewellery made can provide a physical representation of your love and loss. Annual rituals, such as lighting a candle on your child's birthday or anniversary, can also offer a way to keep their memory alive and create a sense of continuity.

At Rhys's day care centre, there lives an apple tree that was named 'Rhysy's apple tree' before he died because the day the children and educators planted it, Rhys stuck his head in the hole so no other children could help plant it. He declared that it was *his* tree. After Rhys died, one of the many calls I received from Lady Gowrie Child Care Centre was from Tania who offered to install a plaque at the base of 'Rhysy's apple tree'. Tania organised the plaque, and Dean and I took a trip to the Central Highlands, a most visited and loved place where the family shack is, to select a Tasmanian dolerite stone to which the plaque is mounted. Dean polished the stone and core drilled a hole under the plaque where we installed a small container with some of Rhys's ashes in it. It was such a beautiful gesture from Tania and the team at Lady Gowrie. A piece of Rhys will always be at his favourite place where he loved exploring with his little friends. After the installation of the plaque, Lady Gowrie held a celebration of Rhys and invited all families and staff to a BBQ where we released balloons. It was a beautiful afternoon for all grieving families to come and show us their support and also be supported by us and the centre. Rhys's death impacted so many lives, especially at Lady Gowrie.

Rhys's plaque and apple tree at the Lady Gowrie day care centre.

Finding New Purpose

Finally, finding a new purpose or project can be a powerful way to cope with grief. Many parents channel their pain into advocacy, charity work, or projects that honour their child's legacy. This sense of purpose can provide direction and meaning, helping you navigate through the darkest days.

Coping with the loss of a child is a lifelong journey. There are days when the pain feels unbearable, but there are also moments of solace and healing. By exploring different coping mechanisms and seeking support, you can find ways to manage your grief and honour your child's memory. Remember, it's okay to ask for help, and it's okay to take this journey one step at a time. You are not alone, and there is hope for healing.

The Role of Professional Help and Therapy

One of my earliest memories following Rhys's death was visiting a psychologist with Dean and being told it was too soon for us to be sitting down and talking about Rhys's death. It was very early on, and I guess we thought they might be able to help, but we were in shock still.

Over the passing years, I visited other psychologists, especially with the impending arrival of our son Elijah in 2018. I found these sessions really helpful for understanding complex trauma, and I was given some tools that I used for quite some time afterwards to decrease my anxiety surrounding mortality and bringing another child into the world.

Then we met Andy.

Our business coach Mick Hawes introduced us to Andy Bryce, an EFT master and trainer. As mentioned previously, EFT stands for 'emotional freedom techniques', a single algorithm tapping technique that's a simplified form of the ancient Chinese system of acupuncture (only without needles), combined with many brilliant facets of neurolinguistic programming. Andy was able to guide Dean and I through a series of EFT sessions together and individually. It released us from the hold of some traumatic memories, images, and physical sensations we were experiencing. This is the most beneficial therapy I've participated in, and I use tapping at home to help with emotional release in day-to-day life.

NAVIGATING THROUGH GRIEF

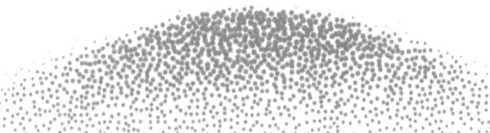

A Breath of Wisdom

Don't neglect self-care – it's an important part of the healing journey.

There's no shame in seeking professional help. There are plenty of support services out there, and it's important that you find the right fit.

Healing from the loss of a child isn't a destination but a lifelong journey.

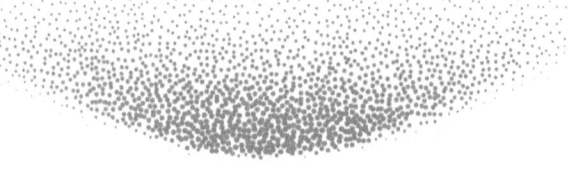

Chapter 6
The Non-Linear Nature of Grief

When Rhys first died, our grief ebbed and flowed in unison. During those early days, possibly the first month or two, our journeys were remarkably similar. But then, things changed.

I started expressing my emotions and grief openly, whereas Dean chose to keep his feelings internalised. This difference led to confusion and misunderstanding, making it challenging to navigate our grief together. The only way we found to bridge this gap was through open discussion. We learnt that we wouldn't always experience the same feelings at the same time, and recognising this was crucial. It led to us giving each other space and protecting each other when we were individually struggling.

Different Journeys Through Grief

I often felt deeply sad and openly emotional, while Dean seemed okay on the surface. He preferred to spend time alone, reflecting and grieving in his own way, often in the shed. This disparity in our grieving processes might have been partly due to gender differences. Men and women often cope with grief differently, and this was certainly true for us. It just comes down to the fact that we're different people, and it was critical that we respected each other's journey.

Dean sought solace in playing a round of golf. It was his way of processing his emotions while also providing a physical release of energy. Seeking normalcy, spending time with friends, and finding routines helped us both. We had to learn to accept the individual nature of our grief, and we still practise giving each other space to grieve. Even now, we allow space for Rhys, despite the routine of daily life.

Discussing our feelings remains crucial. Sometimes, I felt silly bringing up my sadness, thinking enough time had passed. But grief is a lifelong journey, and it doesn't end after the first year, regardless of others' opinions. Those who haven't lost a child can't truly understand.

In the early days, spending time as a family, away from work, was particularly helpful. Trips and holidays provided much-needed respite and helped us support each other. I remember our trip to Noosa a few months after Rhys died.

It felt strange leaving home without him, but it was a vital step in our healing process.

In the early days, I needed time away, whether for a drive or a night alone, for self-reflection. It's brave to take that time, and while I found it challenging, it was necessary.

It's also important not to shut out friends. Even if they don't fully understand, their support is invaluable. They may feel awkward, but they can be a crucial part of your support system.

In those early days, some friends struggled, but the key was to let them know we needed them to be there and to just be themselves. This helped us navigate our grief and find a sense of stability amid the turmoil.

Mums and dads
grieve differently,
and understanding
this is essential.

NAVIGATING THROUGH GRIEF

A Breath of Wisdom

Everyone's journey through
grief is different, although there
will be some similarities.

Don't shut out your support network,
even if they don't fully understand
the situation. You'll need your friends
and family more than ever.

It's important to find your own
path through grief and take the
necessary steps to move forward.

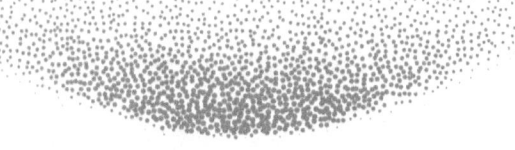

Part 3

The Search for Solace

Chapter 7
Memories and Their Significance

In the aftermath of tragedy, nature often becomes a sanctuary and a source of symbolism for those navigating the depths of grief. Since Rhys died, one of our favourite refuges has been the family shack in the Central Highlands. This place holds treasured memories of us building snowmen, driving along the dirt tracks around the Great Lake, breaking ice-covered puddles, and revelling in the laughter of the kids as we tackled big bumps and slippery paths. "More, more!" Ammi and Rhys would chant. "This one, Dad! Drive through this one!" Dean never needed much encouragement for a bit of off-road adventure in the work ute.

We often piled into the ute and just drove, discovering a favourite loop road that beckoned us to jump out and explore nature's wonders. We named each area we came across – from the

Cricket Pitch to Kangaroo Creek, the Oasis, and Bigpond. This landscape, so familiar to the four of us, now holds a profoundly new meaning.

The Phoenix Tree

A couple of months after Rhys died, we parked in a different spot and set off to explore. Down a steep embankment we ventured, stopping to photograph treasures along the way. At the bottom, we were greeted by a large open space surrounded by forest and dominated by a massive fallen tree. Its size and intricate root system, filled with red dirt and rocks, captivated us. What truly moved us was the sight of a tiny tree growing from the hole left by the fallen giant. This small tree became a powerful symbol of our future, offering us a sense of continuity and permission to move forward with Rhys. We took a photo of it, printed it on canvas, and hung it above our bed as a constant reminder of hope and resilience.

In January 2019, a bushfire ignited by lightning tore through Tasmania's Central Highlands, consuming the bushland we cherished. The fire destroyed our Phoenix Tree and the little tree growing from its base. For a long time, we avoided returning to that hill, exploring other areas instead, too shocked by the devastation to face what was left.

On a boys' trip to the Lakes, Dean revisited the spot. To his surprise, the fallen tree, though charred, had sprouted another, much smaller tree. Despite the fire's destruction, life had found a way to begin anew.

We were stripped bare of everything familiar and cherished. Desperate for answers that didn't exist, we grasped for any hope that could help us keep going. For us, that hope was symbolised by this tree. If we can find a message that encourages us to take one more step forward, that message is real and meaningful. Like a phoenix from the flames.

The Phoenix Tree in Tasmania's Central Highlands.

Some events are
so catastrophic they
irrevocably alter the
life you once knew.

Serenaded in Song

Some moments were a true gift that made us feel so loved and wrapped up in a safe cocoon.

18/9/16

The most amazing thing happened to Mummy and Daddy on Friday night. We went to see one of our favourite singers, Paul Dempsey. He played a song called 'The True Sea'. It is a song that we interpret as the space between people who love each other and are separated by physical presence and time. As he introduced the song he said, 'This song is for Shan and Dean'. Uncle Joel had contacted his managers and asked if Paul could mention us during the show. It is a moment we will never forget. We met Paul after the show and he gave us a big cuddle. We then got to spend some time with him. We showed him photos of you, and he said you were amazing. He signed his new CD and wrote 'For Rhys, Dempsey ♥' It was such a special night. Everything is for you our darling boy.

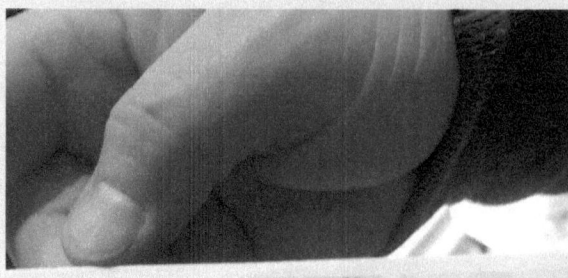

Paul Dempsey's set list.

CD signed for Rhys by Paul Dempsey.

Dean, Shannon, and Paul Dempsey hugging.

An Angel on Earth – Maureen Gilbert

23/8/16

It wasn't a dream. I'm so numb. The Coroner said they had to take you to Hobart for an Autopsy. I told him he would need a car seat to take you there. I felt a bit silly, followed by a feeling of utter despair. I was so worried all day, visualising the car driving on the highway. I just wanted to know what was going on then I received a phone call from a very familiar voice. 'Shannon, darling, I'm here with Rhys.' It was Maureen. She had gone to the hospital and told the Coroner she would be sitting in on your Autopsy. They sent a pastoral care person to support her. She found a chair and put it in the corner. Did you see the white teddy with the blue bow she bought for you? She said she tucked you and teddy in and said goodnight. She said you looked like an angel.

Maureen was like a second mother to me. Growing up with her daughter Joanne as my best friend, I was a part of the furniture at their family home on Wellington Street. The memories of two girls growing up together, supported and loved by our parents, are cherished. Life seemed simpler in the '80s and '90s.

One of my earliest memories of Mo is her studying at the University of Tasmania while still giving her all to her three children. Wellington Street was a comforting, warm place where there was always a meal of chops, vegetables, and beans for anyone who walked through the back door. Maureen welcomed everyone with open arms, especially us teenagers who often didn't know when to leave. Nothing was ever too much trouble for her.

When Rhys died, Maureen was living in Hobart, working as a detective constable in the Hobart Criminal Investigation Branch (CIB). She called me from the morgue. "Shannon, I'm here with Rhys," she said. "I'll be sitting in on the autopsy if that's okay with you and Dean. I just don't want him to be alone. I'll let you know when it's over." I burst into tears. My anxiety eased, and all the tension and fear melted away. She had a spiritual presence, and her beautiful Irish accent still brings me peace when I think of that conversation.

A couple of hours later, she called again. "Shannon, it's done. I've tucked him in and given him a little teddy to cuddle." The same teddy we placed with Rhys in his coffin along with his few favourite comforts.

In 2018, we lost a beautiful soul who blessed everyone she met. I know she's up in heaven, spoiling Rhys and loving him unconditionally.

Rest peacefully, sweetest lady. You were truly an angel who walked this earth x

THE SEARCH FOR SOLACE

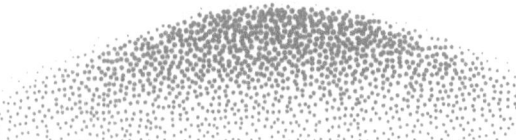

A Breath of Wisdom

Nature can become both a sanctuary
and a source of symbolism.

Life often finds a way to begin anew.

Just one loving and supportive person
can make a world of difference.

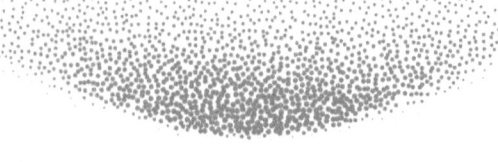

Chapter 8
Symbolism and Signs

Overwhelming grief can make the world seem bleak and devoid of purpose. Grand gestures and monumental achievements often feel insignificant. However, it's often in the small things, the seemingly inconsequential moments and subtle details, that we find profound meaning.

Finding Meaning in the Small Things, Discovering Purpose

While grief can make it challenging to appreciate the small joys of daily life, these moments often hold significant meaning and can be a source of comfort and connection. Practising mindfulness was something very new to me after Rhys died. It helped me become more attuned to the small moments found in daily life. The glimmers, the micro-moments of joy. Whether it was savouring a cup of tea or feeling the warmth of sunlight on my skin, being present in these moments offered a sense of peace, connection, and stillness.

I established small daily rituals to provide structure and a sense of normalcy that I so desperately sought. I dedicated time to journalling, went to the gym, video called my brother, took family walks, or met a friend for coffee. Occasionally, I would light a candle for Rhys. I volunteered so much time to parent help at school. Being close to Ammi helped, seeing her playing and laughing with her friends. Conversations with 6-year-olds are a wonderful distraction and really brought me so much joy. These rituals offered a sense of continuity and routine, and became opportunities for reflection and gratitude.

Creating Personal Rituals

Personal rituals can help you honour your child's memory and find meaning in everyday life. These rituals can be tailored to your preferences and provide a way to connect with your child in a meaningful way.

Memory projects. Create a memory project that reflects your child's spirit. This could be a scrapbook, a photo album, or a digital collection of photos or slideshows. Revisiting these projects can provide a sense of closeness and allow you to celebrate your child's life. Having a digital slideshow of Rhys's photos was an easy way to share moments with him. I'd play his favourite songs, watch the slideshow, and just cry, laugh, and be with my boy. I needed these tools to trigger my grief at times, especially in the early days when I found it hard to release my emotions.

Legacy acts. Consider engaging in acts of kindness or charity. Whether it's volunteering, making a donation, or supporting a cause, these acts can be a meaningful way to honour your child. It doesn't need to be something huge, just something that may bring you comfort and honour.

Commemorative traditions. Develop traditions that commemorate your child on special occasions or anniversaries. This could include planting a tree, releasing balloons, or participating in an annual event that holds significance. There are so many options and ideas. Most of our ideas came from Google searches or asking friends and family. Some people we know instigated ideas for us, which was really appreciated.

Finding Meaning in Everyday Objects

Sometimes, everyday objects can hold deep meaning and provide comfort. By focusing on these objects, you can find solace and connection.

Keepsakes. Cherish keepsakes that remind you of your child, such as a piece of clothing, a favourite toy, a special letter, or some paintings. These objects can often be disregarded before child loss is experienced. I can't express how important these objects are and continue to be for our children. Rhys's passing brought a whole new meaning to the order of importance of material possessions.

Personal spaces. Create a personal space in your home that honours your child. This might include a dedicated shelf, or a cosy corner where you can reflect and remember. Our space for Rhys has evolved over the years. Initially, his bedroom was his space. We had removed his bed and replaced it with a couch. Everything else remained untouched until the arrival of Elijah in our little home, which meant Rhys's room transformed into a nursery, and the heart-wrenching job of packing up Rhys's belongings began. This is when we started filling 'Rhysy's cabinet' with all his treasures and favourite things. When we sold our place, Rhysy's cabinet was meticulously packed down and was reinvented in our new home in the spare room with the same couch. It's a beautiful, quiet space we've created.

Sensory triggers. Pay attention to sensory triggers, such as scents, sounds, and textures, that remind you of your child. Just today, I put on a new deodorant, which I must have been using around the time Rhys died. This morning, I was taken back to that moment from the smell of the deodorant. Perfume, bubble bath, there are so many sensory triggers that still pop up regularly. These triggers can provide a sense of comfort, but they can also catch you off guard.

Rediscovering Gratitude

Gratitude is tough to comprehend for a long time following the loss of a child. Finding things to be grateful for can be a struggle. In my case, at the beginning, gratitude was the last thing on my mind. I was angry and felt isolated. I was resentful towards a lot of people, especially on social media, who had no regard for just how lucky they were. The whinging and negativity of others affected me. I woke up one day and realised that the only person putting me through such negativity was me, and it had to stop. I removed myself from social media for a short time to collect myself. There are times people still grind my gears, but I recognise the signs, and I choose to put my energy into the amazing people around me.

Given time, I found gratitude for small things, and it can be a powerful tool for finding meaning and shifting your perspective.

There's a lot I'm grateful for now, including the perspective on life that Rhys has gifted us, which we teach to our children. Fortunately, not many people we know have had the chance to see life from the perspective of a bereaved parent. While some moments can be incredibly challenging, there are also profoundly joyful moments that few others have the opportunity to experience.

Gratitude journalling. Keep a gratitude journal where you write down small things you appreciate each day. When I'm struggling, first thing each morning as part of my success ritual, I write in my journal three things I'm grateful for. This practice can help you recognise the positive aspects of your life and find meaning in everyday moments.

Sharing gratitude. Share your feelings of gratitude with others. Expressing thanks to those who support you can strengthen your relationships and create a sense of connection.

Finding Purpose Through the Small Things

Finding meaning in the small things after child loss isn't about diminishing the significance of your grief but about discovering moments of solace and connection amid the pain. By embracing

Remember that each small moment and gesture holds the potential for profound significance.

daily rituals, simple pleasures, and personal projects, you can create a new sense of purpose and honour your child's memory in meaningful ways.

By focusing on these moments, you can find comfort, connection, and a renewed sense of purpose in the midst of your grief. Your child's memory can inspire you to find beauty and meaning in the small things, offering a path towards healing.

From Deep Despair Comes Significant Joy

I was introduced to the phrase, "From deep despair comes significant joy" by a wonderful psychologist. It reflects the idea that profound suffering or hardship can sometimes lead to profound personal growth and a heightened appreciation of life.

When people endure intense grief or difficulty, they often emerge with a deeper understanding of themselves and their capacity for resilience. This transformative process can lead to a renewed sense of joy and fulfilment that might not have been possible without experiencing the depth of their struggle. Essentially, the contrast between despair and joy can amplify their appreciation, highlighting the potential for growth and healing, even in the wake of great pain. It's a phrase I really resonate with, and it always stays with me on my journey.

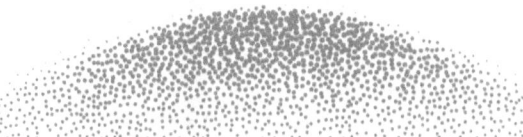

A Breath of Wisdom

Practising mindfulness can help
you recognise and acknowledge
the glimmers of joy in life.

Through personal rituals and projects,
you can honour your child's memory
and preserve their legacy.

As difficult as it might be to
believe at first, from deep
despair comes significant joy.

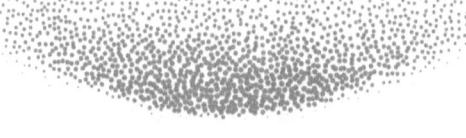

Chapter 9
Healing Through Exploration

Nature has a unique ability to offer calm and perspective in times of emotional turmoil and pain. Spending time in natural environments can reduce stress, lower blood pressure, and improve mood, all of which can be incredibly beneficial when coping with grief. For me, taking short walks alone or with others provided a sense of freedom. A change-up in breath rhythm and movement disrupts thought patterns and provides some respite from the heavy weight of one's grief. I sought relief from my grief at the gym. Pushing myself physically was a welcome distraction from certain thought and behaviour patterns.

When Rhys died, friends gifted plants to us. We received a magnolia tree (among a multitude of other thoughtful gifts) named 'Little Gem' and a white rose bush named 'Mother's Love'. People were so thoughtful; it still amazes me to this day.

There were a lot of young children at Rhys's funeral. Friends of Amalie and children of parents who are our dear friends. Our beautiful friend brought DIY fairy garden kits with her to keep the children busy at the wake. It was such a beautiful gesture and took the pressure off the children, allowing them to just be kids in a very intense setting.

A Shift in Perception

After loss, it's common to notice a shift in how we perceive colours. What once might have seemed ordinary now appears extraordinary. This intensified perception can be both overwhelming and comforting. Colours might seem more vivid and intricate, as if nature is reaching out to offer a new form of connection.

Sensory experiences – the feel of the earth underfoot, the smell of fresh pine, the sight of a blooming flower – can ground you in the present moment and provide a gentle respite from the intensity of your emotions. These inputs can act as anchors, pulling you away from the overwhelming waves of grief and helping you reconnect with the here and now. For me, lying on grass and looking up at the sky brought relief. The smell of flowers and freshly cut grass, observing new flowers blooming – my senses were heightened in the early days. These simple pleasures continue to bring me joy and since the day Rhys died, I've had a new-found appreciation for nature.

This heightened sensory experience offers a new way to connect with the world around you and find moments of beauty. Embracing these enhanced senses can be part of the bigger picture of healing. Engage with nature, and let it be a source of comfort.

In time, this new perspective on nature might help you find meaning, allowing you to honour your child's memory in a way that feels deeply personal. By embracing the experiences that follow loss, you may discover a new sense of appreciation for the world and a deeper connection to the life that surrounds you.

Building Connections, Seizing Opportunities, and Taking Risks After Child Loss

In the aftermath of losing a child, it's natural to retreat and avoid new experiences. Yet, in this period of deep mourning, there lies an opportunity to reshape your life and honour your child's memory in transformative ways.

Create New Connections, Maintain Old Ones

Grief for me is isolating. It definitely felt easier to withdraw from social interactions. However, building new connections can provide a vital source of support and introduce fresh perspectives into your life.

Connecting with others who have experienced similar losses can be incredibly validating. As mentioned previously, support groups, both in-person and online, offer a space where you can share your feelings and hear others' stories. These groups can help you feel less alone and provide practical advice on navigating grief.

Engage in activities or hobbies that interest you. Grab a friend and try new things. Whether it's joining a restaurant club, taking a cooking class, attending a yoga retreat, or participating in community events, these settings offer opportunities to meet new people. Shared interests can provide a foundation for new friendships and help you feel reconnected to the world.

Channelling your energy into helping others can create meaningful connections and provide a sense of purpose. I spent a lot of my time bringing Rally for Rhys Foundation to life, raising funds for bereaved families, and it brought me so much connection and sense of achievement. We also collaborated as a foundation with Love Your Sister to raise funds for cancer.

You never know where an undertaking can lead you. Both Rally for Rhys and the Love Your Sister fundie were such rewarding opportunities. Helping others can also foster a supportive network and bring new, positive interactions into your life.

Say Yes to More Opportunities

Grief can make it difficult to embrace new experiences. The idea of venturing out of your comfort zone may seem daunting, but saying yes to more opportunities, when you feel you're ready, can open doors.

While it might be challenging, try to attend social gatherings or events. It took me a long time to feel like socialising because being in a social setting where people were relaxed and having fun felt like everyone had forgotten about Rhys. This was so far from the truth, but it was how I felt at the time. So, even if you don't feel like socialising, just being around others can help you feel more engaged with life. Staying at a gathering or event for only a short time is okay too. Gradually, these interactions may become more enjoyable and less taxing.

Allow yourself to explore interests or activities you've always been curious about. Whether it's taking a class, travelling to a new place, travelling more frequently if time and money allow, or learning a new skill, embracing new experiences can be a way to honour your child's memory by living fully. This was a really important avenue for me, honouring Rhys's life by living because he wasn't given the chance to grow up and live life to the fullest himself.

If friends or family invite you to events, try to accept their invitations, even if you're hesitant. These moments can provide a welcome distraction and remind you of the support network around you. With a light-hearted approach, small doses of invites and events can be really rewarding.

Start with small, manageable goals to push yourself gently outside of your comfort zone. As you achieve these goals, you'll build confidence and resilience, making it easier to embrace larger opportunities. Remember, if you said yes but when the time comes you can't step out the door, that's okay too. Try and try again. Baby steps are better than no steps at all. Be kind to yourself.

Take Necessary Risks
After a significant loss, taking risks can feel overwhelming. However, embracing calculated risks can lead to personal growth and a renewed sense of purpose. If there's something you've always wanted to do but never had the chance, now might be the time to pursue it. Whether it's starting a new business, writing a book, or creating art, taking the leap to follow your passions can be a powerful way to honour your child's memory and find fulfilment. It's important to seek advice and/or coaching if required so taking the leap doesn't end up causing further stress and heartache. Do it right the first time and feel supported.

Identify areas of your life where you've been playing it safe and consider taking small risks. This could mean speaking up in a meeting, sharing your story with others, or exploring new career opportunities. Each risk can help you grow and build resilience.

By actively engaging with the world and stepping outside your comfort zone, you honour your child's memory by living a life that's rich with meaning and connection.

Each new relationship, opportunity, and risk taken is a testament to your strength and resilience.

I certainly found my voice after Rhys's passing. I think, in a way, I found my confidence and took a more 'what have you got to lose' mentality, in a positive, non-destructive way.

Sometimes, taking risks involves embracing change. It should involve a lot of thought and assessment, but it might mean moving to a new place, changing jobs, or rethinking your daily routine. Change can be challenging, but it can also bring new opportunities for growth and connection.

Be gentle with yourself as you navigate new risks and opportunities. It's important to acknowledge that taking risks can be intimidating and setbacks are a normal part of the process. Practise self-compassion and recognise your efforts, no matter the outcome. Just taking one step in front of the other could be your greatest achievement for the day, and it needs to be celebrated.

Finding Balance and Purpose

In the journey of building new connections, embracing opportunities, and taking risks, it's all about finding a balance that feels right for you. Remember that healing isn't about rushing through the process but about finding ways to move forward at your own pace.

As you navigate this journey, remember that it's okay to take small steps and every effort you make is a step towards healing.

Your child's memory can inspire you to live a life filled with connection, possibility, and courage. I had a poster given to me when Rhys died, which sat in our lounge room below the TV. It said, "Bravery and boldness are a work of art." It takes courage to be brave and bold. It's easier for some than others, and that's okay.

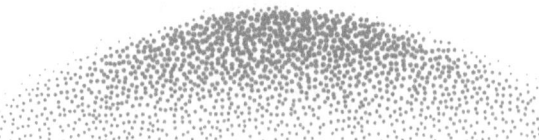

A Breath of Wisdom

Following loss, shifts in perception can occur – for example, colours may seem more vivid – which can be confronting.

As part of the healing journey, it's important to create new connections, seize opportunities, and take necessary risks.

Healing should occur at your own pace, even if that means taking only small steps forward.

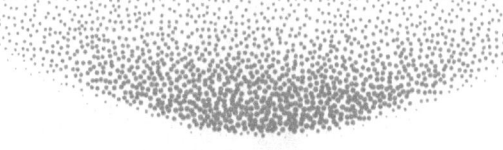

Part 4

Connection

Chapter 10
The Foundations of Family

The loss of a child is an unthinkable tragedy that can shake the very foundation of a family. It's a wound that cuts deep, often leaving behind a sense of hopelessness, anger, and confusion. In the wake of such a loss, families may find themselves grappling with how to move forward, how to reconnect, and how to rebuild their lives in the absence of their beloved child.

When a family loses a child, the very bedrock of their existence is shattered. The roles within the family dynamic may feel skewed or completely upended. Bereaved parents often experience a profound sense of guilt and helplessness; siblings may feel forgotten or overwhelmed with their own grief, and the once familiar home can suddenly seem unfamiliar and cold. It's important to understand that these feelings are natural and to acknowledge the magnitude of the loss. The family foundation isn't shattered beyond repair; it's simply damaged, and with time and care, it can be mended.

Embracing Vulnerability

The process of rebuilding a family after loss requires a deep level of vulnerability from each family member. This vulnerability isn't a sign of weakness but rather a crucial aspect of healing. I recall us having to learn to verbally express our feelings to each other and to encourage Amalie to do the same, and it felt unnatural. Expressing our grief openly was confronting, on top of feeling so exposed already. It was a heavy weight to carry, and most of the time it was easier to suppress our feelings. We had to learn to let ourselves cry, be angry, be alone, and feel lost. Creating a space where everyone feels safe to share their emotions without judgment fosters a stronger, more connected family unit.

Amalie was 5 years old when Rhys died. We had to allow space for her to communicate her sadness in her own way. She needed time and space for her grief to evolve and develop its own complexity and weight. Amalie knew that Rhys had died and wasn't coming back but as she aged, the complexity and weight of his death really showed in her grief.

When family members isolate themselves emotionally, the foundation of the family becomes even more fragile. Being open with each other helps prevent isolation, which is a common response to grief. But when we came together in our vulnerability, we began to rebuild trust, understanding, and mutual support – key elements of a strong family foundation.

Redefining Family Roles

In the aftermath of child loss, it's natural for family roles to shift. I know, as parents, we can feel a void where our caregiving instincts used to be. Siblings might feel an increased pressure to fill the gap left by the lost child. These shifts can create additional stress and confusion within the family.

To rebuild the family foundation, it's essential to openly discuss these role changes and redefine them in a way that honours the family's current needs. We didn't do this, and, looking back, I felt lost, as the balance was out. Three family members is a different dynamic from four. I had been nurturing Rhys as a 2-year-old child. Although Amalie was only 5 years old when Rhys died, she was always mature for her age, and I very suddenly lost so many daily responsibilities.

What might it look like to discuss role changes? When I look back, it might involve parents rediscovering their roles as partners to each other or focusing on nurturing the surviving children in new ways. Siblings might take on new responsibilities, or perhaps the family collectively decides to engage in activities that foster connection and healing. It's important that these roles are defined through communication and mutual agreement, rather than assumed out of a sense of obligation or guilt.

Reconnecting Through Shared Memories

Memories of the lost child can be both painful and comforting. It's common for families to struggle with how to keep their child's memory alive without feeling overwhelmed by sorrow. One way to rebuild the family's foundation is by intentionally creating rituals or practices that honour the child's memory while also fostering connection among family members. This could be something as simple as setting aside time each week to share stories about the child or creating a special space in the home dedicated to their memory. Some families find comfort in celebrating the child's birthday each year or engaging in acts of kindness in their name.

We looked at photos together, listened to Rhys's favourite songs, and discussed funny memories, but all in small amounts. It was an enjoyable but painful experience. My brother Joel created 'Rhys Random Act of Kindness' cards, which we used and encouraged family and friends on social media to use, especially on Rhys's birthday or anniversary. Rhys loved Mr Bean, so we asked

These shared memories and rituals serve as a bridge between the past and the present, allowing the family to feel connected to their child while also strengthening their bond with each other.

family and friends to change their profile picture on Facebook to a picture of Mr Bean on Rhys's anniversary. They were small tokens that really spread the love and kept Rhys's spirit alive.

Download your own Rhys Random Act of Kindness cards.
rallyforrhys.com.au/wp-content/uploads/2018/01/RAOK_Rhys_A4x4.pdf

Seeking Support

Finally, it's important to acknowledge that rebuilding a family after child loss isn't something that can be done alone. Seeking support from outside the family – whether through counselling, support groups, or spiritual guidance – can provide valuable perspectives and tools for healing. Sometimes, it takes an external voice to help the family see the path forward or to remind them that they're not alone in their grief. Support groups, in particular, can offer a sense of community and understanding that are invaluable during the grieving process. Connecting with others who have experienced similar losses can provide comfort and insights that are difficult to find elsewhere. It's a reminder that while each family's journey is unique, they don't have to walk it alone. It's important not to seek support too early, like we did. Take your time and reach out when you feel ready, not when others think you're ready.

Rebuilding the foundations of family after the loss of a child is one of the most challenging journeys a family can face. It requires patience, compassion, and a willingness to embrace both the pain and the possibility of healing. By understanding the impact of the loss, embracing vulnerability, redefining family roles, reconnecting through shared memories, finding new purpose, and seeking support when ready, families can begin to lay the groundwork for a future that, while forever changed, can still be filled with love, connection, and hope.

This chapter, and this book as a whole, isn't about forgetting or moving on; it's about honouring our children while finding a way to live and love in their absence. The foundation may have cracked, but with time, care, and effort, it can be rebuilt, stronger and more resilient than before. It certainly has happened this way for us.

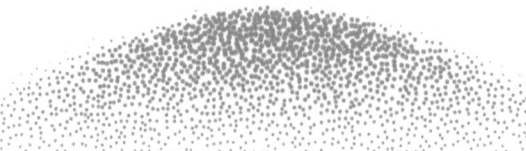

A Breath of Wisdom

Vulnerability isn't a sign of weakness but a necessary part of healing.

Discuss and redefine roles within the family if necessary.

Don't hesitate to seek support outside of the family.

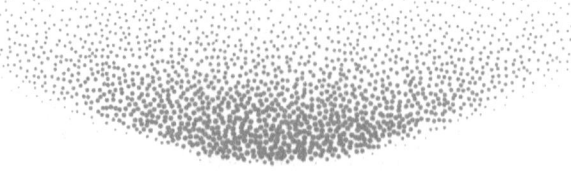

Chapter 11

Support Networks, and the Elephant in the Room

Close friends carry a lot of pressure when a friend's child dies. Many friendships fade because it can just be too difficult to know what to say. If you're a friend of a bereaved parent, it's important to know that you actually don't need to know what to say. The most important thing to do is just be present. It's okay to say, "I don't know what to say. I'm sorry, I can't imagine how hard it is." In my experience, this shows the biggest effort has already been made by just showing up. We lost a lot of close friends when Rhys died, and we don't blame those people. I've been in their shoes. I've thought, *It's too soon to call. Now it's too late. They have so many other friends, they don't need me. I don't want to feel like I'm intruding. What if they cry? What if I say the wrong thing?*

There are so many hesitations that may stop you from picking up the phone. It's a tough position to be in, but I believe it's important to rip off the bandaid, send a message, and ask if they need anything or if there's a good time to chat or visit. They're still the same person and once the funeral is over and the family has returned home, they may be lost and just need a friend. Don't ever worry about saying their child's name. You aren't sparking a painful memory; they think of their child every waking moment. You're not causing any further pain or damage. If they cry, you're helping to release grief. It's okay to cry with them. Losing a child is one of the worst things that can happen to a human being. Be kind, humble, and vulnerable. It will be appreciated and remembered forever.

28/8/16

I miss you bubba. Today was a lovely day. We are staying strong. I pine for you, but I know you are with me every second of the day. Please stay in our hearts. Don't you get too busy playing that you forget to look after us. Uncle Ben and Morgan are here to help us. They took us shopping to find an outfit for Ammi to wear to your celebration. It was nice to get out of the house although it felt like the world was spinning, I felt so dizzy. Morgan found a beautiful dress and little cape for Ammi. She will look like a princess. You always thought she was a princess, you idolised her every move.

CONNECTION

Uncle Ben came with us to see you at the funeral home today. He wanted to give you his blessing and let you know that he would look after us for you. He bought an army teddy for you and he gave you his medals. He came into our lives for a reason Rhys. Him and Morgs. I have no doubt he will look after us and Ammi for the rest of our lives. I know Natasha and Teena are taking good care of you at Finneys. I feel less worried and sad knowing they are there with you. Sweet dreams bubba xx

2/9/16

Ken, Laura, Ella and Ned came tonight for dinner. It was lovely to see them, but we missed you so much. Ned has taken spot, your toy from The Good Dinosaur. Remember watching that movie with Ammi, Ella and Ned on the couch eating ice-cream? Ned will love and cherish your toy as much as he loves you.

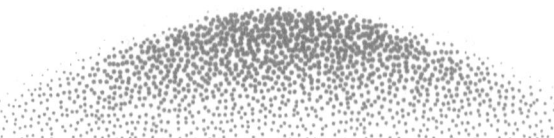

A Breath of Wisdom

If you're the friend of a bereaved parent, it's okay if you don't know what to say. Just be present and offer your support.

Don't hesitate to pick up the phone – your friend likely needs you more than you know.

By speaking their child's name, you're not causing the parents further pain. They're already thinking of their child every waking moment.

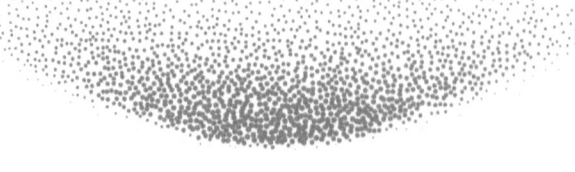

Chapter 12
Personal Reflections and Journalling

As you know, I started writing to Rhys on the day he died. I was gifted a beautiful journal from my dearest friend Laura, and I remember kneeling at the end of my bed to write to Rhys that night.

With a house full of family and friends, it was just a short entry and the most I could manage that day.

22/8/16
Goodnight sweet baby. Mummy and Daddy love you with all our hearts. Eee Eee is sleeping in our bed tonight. Please watch over us all including Amalie.

Eee Eee, Rhys's favourite toy monkey, is still positioned on the head of our bed.

Journal gifted to Shannon from Laura.

It took me a very long time to look back over the content in my journal to Rhys, which is the main reason why it took me 8 years to write this book. When I read back through the journal, my heart breaks all over again. I remember being so utterly scared of the future. I can feel my desperation in the tone of my journal entries. I was protecting Rhys, reassuring him we were okay, pleading with him to stay with us. I also wrote about glimmers of hope and how one day we would be okay. I captured moments of joy and described how the world looked different now that Rhys was gone.

The Role of Writing in Healing

In the early days, writing in my journal to Rhys nearly every day became a ritual, and it was one of a few activities that kept me going. As time went on, entries became weekly, then monthly. I remember feeling guilty because I hadn't journalled in weeks, but it was important to me to not make it a chore and to pick up the journal if I felt I needed to say something to Rhys. Writing emerged as a powerful ally. It was always there if I needed it. It was a release and a dumping ground for my thoughts. For me, writing was a profound act of healing and transformation.

Emotions often feel too vast and chaotic to contain, like you're stuck in a cyclone. Everything is fuzzy, chaotic, overwhelming, and scary. Writing offers a structured way to express these emotions, making them more manageable and less overwhelming.

Journalling is one of the most accessible and therapeutic forms of writing. It allows you to freely explore your thoughts and feelings without judgement. This private space can become a sanctuary where you can grapple with the complexities of your grief, from the raw and painful to the tender and nostalgic.

Finding Your Voice

In the wake of Rhys's death, my identity was irrevocably altered. Even though the content of my journal was between me and

By articulating your grief, you not only validate your feelings but also create a space where your emotions can be processed and eventually understood.

Rhys, writing became a tool for rediscovering and reclaiming my voice. When I wrote about Rhys and my personal experience, I honoured his memory and also asserted my own identity in the midst of change.

My words to Rhys were healing. They gave me a way to maintain a connection with him. I expressed things left unsaid, and I celebrated his life with him. Until now, I hadn't shared my journal entries, but I'm sharing them now in hope of helping others.

Your journal entries don't have to be shared with anyone; they're meant for you, as a means to navigate your emotions and keep the bond alive.

Structuring the Chaos

Grief can feel like a storm that uproots everything in its path. Writing helps to impose some order on the chaos. By organising my thoughts and emotions on paper, I created a narrative that helped me make some sense of my experience.

Writing prompts can be a useful tool if you're struggling with where to begin. Prompts such as, "One memory of my child that brings me comfort is…" or, "I can't shake the feeling of despair today, and that makes me feel…" can guide you in expressing specific aspects of your grief. Over time, this practice can help you gain perspective and find meaning in your journey.

Healing Through Reflection

As mentioned earlier in this chapter, looking back on the contents of my journal is quite profound and is an important part of the healing process. As I looked back on my journal entries, I noticed changes in my thoughts and feelings. This reflection offered insights into my healing process and showed me how life has changed since the early stages of my grief.

Grief journals are particularly valuable because they provide a record of your emotional journey. They allow you to track your progress, recognise patterns, and identify moments of growth. This ongoing dialogue with yourself can be a source of comfort and reassurance.

Connecting with Others

Writing doesn't have to be a solitary activity. Sharing your writing with others, whether through support groups, blogs, or social media, can create connections with those who understand your experience. I established a Facebook page where I would share photos and memories. The posts are few and far between these days, as I post about Rhys on my personal page now, but it was certainly helpful at the start of our child loss journey. The page also gave friends and support people a place to offer support and love.

Public writing, such as contributing to a blog or a book, can be a way to turn your pain into something that helps others. By sharing your story, you can offer support and solace to others who are navigating similar experiences. This was something I couldn't find when Rhys died, hence the reason I'm writing this book. All books I found back then were very Americanised, religious, or overly cathartic and made me feel so much worse. Getting your thoughts onto paper with the support of a great publishing team can, in turn, be a powerful part of your own healing process as well.

Creative Outlets and Rituals

In addition to journalling and reflective writing, creative writing can also play a role in healing. Poetry, stories, and essays allow you to explore your emotions in different and often cathartic ways. Creative writing can be a means of expressing feelings that are difficult to articulate otherwise. While I haven't tried this yet, I'm really interested in giving it a go and adding it to my journal.

Rituals involving writing, such as releasing a balloon with a letter attached or creating a scrapbook of memories, can also be comforting. These rituals provide a tangible way to honour your child and acknowledge your ongoing grief. On Rhys's anniversary one year, Dean and I went to the local bookshop and bought a copy of Rhys's favourite book, *We're Going on a Bear Hunt* by Michael Rosen, and we wrote inside the cover…

We left the book at the store and asked them to gift it to the next customer who came in with a child to buy a book.

Rituals including balloons, flowers, and writing in Rhys's favourite book to gift to another child.

Embrace the Process

It's important to remember that writing is a process, not a solution. It won't erase your grief or replace what was lost, but it can be a powerful tool for navigating and making sense of your emotions. Be patient with yourself and with the process. There's no right or wrong way to write about your grief – there's only your way. If you're like me, it can feel unnatural at first. But as time went on, it became a ritual that brought me peace and made me feel closer to Rhys. It gave me confidence in many areas, like I was seeking justification from Rhys when I wrote about things I was going to do or how I was feeling. It was a great outlet.

It's important to allow yourself to write without expectation. Your words may be raw, disjointed, or even chaotic, and that's perfectly okay. I repeated myself a lot in the journal. The act of writing itself is what's most important – the act of confronting and expressing your emotions in a way that feels right for you. It's not supposed to be an award-winning piece of literature. It's private, and it belongs to no one but you.

Significant Dates and Anniversaries

At the time of writing this, Rhys's 8-year anniversary of his death has recently come and gone. Every year on 22 August, Dean and I spend the day together and generally make plans on the day. It's too overwhelming to plan in the lead-up because, commonly, the lead-up is the most horrendous time in grief, and it's hard enough to function, let alone come up with ideas of what to do. If I'm quite honest, the entire month of August (fondly renamed by close friends as 'Poogust') is horrible. I'm full of anxiety;

everything I do takes effort; I can't get enough sleep. In August, I guess my grief consumes me. I don't have the energy to fight it and stay positive, and I've learnt to just accept it. Dean and I run our own business, which is demanding at the best of times but come August, my appointments are kept to a minimum, and I take on other tasks that are less stressful and I know I can handle.

Frankly, 22 August haunts us to the core. Although memories of that day come and go regularly, on that day they flood back in. The first couple of years were bad, but it's more manageable now, helped by EFT therapy addressing memories and images etched in my mind from that day. In 2024, I was full of frustration, which was a relatively new emotion for me to experience on 22 August, and it caught me by surprise. All I did was accept the way I was feeling and made sure I didn't take out my frustration on others.

An interesting fact – the day after 22 August is always worse! While the 22nd has always been a bittersweet day, celebrating Rhys and honouring him, the 23rd is tough, as it signifies the start of another long, heavy year without Rhys. I can pretty much write off my mood and productivity until 1 September. Once Poogust is over, spring has usually sprung, bringing new hopes and opportunities. Sometimes, though, optimism is nowhere to be found, so I ride it out and hope for the best because I'm a realist and sometimes positivity isn't welcome! Swings and roundabouts, I guess.

CONNECTION

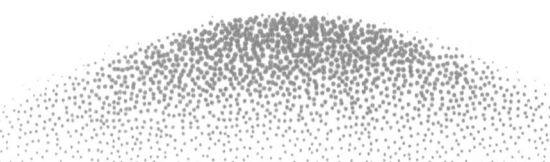

A Breath of Wisdom

Consider journalling as a release for
your thoughts and emotions, a way
to bring structure to the chaos.

Writing can be a tool for rediscovering
and reclaiming your voice and identity.

Other creative endeavours
can also help with the grieving
process. Do what works for you.

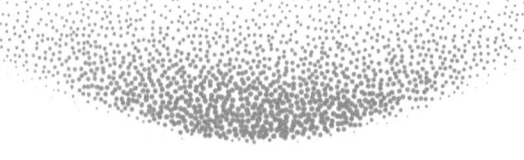

Part 5

Living with Loss

Chapter 13

Embracing a New Normal

After the initial shock and intense grief subside, there comes a time when you must navigate a new normal. This new reality isn't something you choose but rather something you must learn to accept and integrate into your life. Simple routines like getting out of bed, going to work, and engaging in social activities can feel daunting. Yet, slowly, you begin to find a rhythm, even if it feels different from before.

Adjusting to this new normal involves acknowledging the permanent change that loss brings. It's about finding a balance between honouring your child's memory and continuing to live your life. This process is unique for everyone, and there's no right or wrong way to do it.

Work

We were lucky enough to have the flexibility of running our own business, but this also put so much pressure on Dean to keep the business running. When Rhys died, we had a couple of guys working for us. The morning of Rhys's death, like every Monday morning, they showed up for work at our house and were faced with a sea of ambulances, police, and coroners. Our longest serving team member was there that day as an apprentice and is now a senior member of our team. I remember briefly speaking with him many years ago about that day, but recently we relived it together. He said he remembered seeing Dean that morning and knowing something was really wrong. He thought I had died but just grabbed what he needed for the day and drove to the site to start work. I can't imagine how distressing it must have been for our guys, not knowing what was happening.

So, while we had the flexibility of not working full days, Dean still had to quote work to keep the boys busy, and I had administration to attend to. The day Rhys died, I had to sit at the computer and process payroll. It's a really bad memory, and I'm not sure everyone was paid correctly that day. Months went by and while we thought we were doing a great job just to function and keep the bills paid, we started to struggle financially as the business took the financial toll of errors, non-productivity, and poor management. We came to a crossroads – I remember it well. We decided to keep going and claw our way back. After thirteen years of trading, with support and guidance and an enormous amount of grit and determination, we're operating a very successful construction company. We're so proud of how we've turned our business around.

Not everyone has the flexibility of running their own business. While most people will have some time off, they'll likely need to return to work soon. I know of a local business that managed the return of a newly bereaved parent exceptionally well. On their first day back, the company arranged a meeting to discuss their needs and preferences for how they wanted to be treated. This thoughtful approach demonstrated that the employee was valued and respected, and it provided a chance for them to communicate their personal preferences regarding how their situation should be handled. Since everyone's needs are different, some might prefer colleagues to mention their child's name, while others might not want any discussion unless initiated by themselves. Aligning everyone's understanding helps create a supportive and comfortable environment. Additionally, it's crucial for bereaved parents to be aware of any available workplace support. In my experience with larger companies, there are often employee support services that cover initial counselling sessions with an external therapist. This is a supportive option that businesses could consider offering to their employees.

Families

When a parent loses a child, the pressure on grandparents, uncles, and aunts can be immense, as they grapple with their own grief while also trying to support the grieving parents. These relatives may feel a profound sense of helplessness and sorrow, knowing that their loved ones are enduring unimaginable pain. The weight of this emotional burden can be compounded by the expectation to provide comfort and stability, despite their own heartache. They often find themselves in a delicate position, trying to balance their personal grief with the need to offer practical support, emotional solace, and a semblance of normalcy to the bereaved parents, who may be overwhelmed by their loss.

One of my most comforting memories is from the day after Rhys's death. All of our immediate family, including our siblings, plus aunties and uncles who had flown from mainland Australia, gathered for a meal in our tiny house.

Dinner with close family following Rhys's death.

In that moment, I knew it was a lifelong journey we were about to face without Rhys, but I also knew we would be okay.

I remember the warmth and safety of the presence of each person there like it was yesterday.

We're constantly supported by our families, and we're so lucky to have a strong network. For bereaved parents who lack a strong family network, finding support can be particularly challenging, but there are several resources and avenues they can explore. Community support groups and counselling services offer a space where you can connect with others who have experienced similar losses, providing both emotional support and practical advice. Online forums and social media groups dedicated to grief and loss can also be valuable, offering a sense of community and understanding from people who are geographically dispersed but share comparable experiences. Additionally, professional therapists specialising in grief counselling can offer both immediate support and long-term resources, helping parents build a supportive network during an incredibly difficult time.

Friendships

Losing a child often leads to the unanticipated challenge of losing friends. Grieving parents might experience this shift because some people feel uncomfortable around them, unsure of how to offer support, or find it difficult to engage with the intense emotions surrounding the loss. Friends who once seemed close may distance themselves, unintentionally or otherwise, due to their own discomfort or fear of saying the wrong thing. This distancing can compound the bereaved parents' feelings of isolation and loneliness, making an already devastating experience even more painful. The absence of these social connections can leave parents feeling unsupported and abandoned during a time when they most need empathy and companionship.

For friends and acquaintances, the act of distancing themselves can also have emotional repercussions. They might struggle with their own feelings of guilt or helplessness, knowing they're not providing the support they wish they could. The disconnect can lead to unresolved feelings and strained relationships, where the inability to communicate openly about the loss creates a barrier to mutual understanding and healing. In the long run, both the bereaved and those who withdraw can be left with a sense of unresolved loss and missed opportunities for connection and support. It highlights the importance of open communication and compassion in the face of grief, and it's tough – there's no denying that it's difficult.

I've been in both sets of shoes. I had a friend lose her husband suddenly. At his funeral, I was actually pregnant with Rhys. Time went on, and the thoughts started to consume me. *It's too soon to call her, she'll have people around her. What if I say the wrong thing? She won't want me to support her, I don't know how she feels.* I let my own hesitations take over when what I should have done was put her first. It wasn't about me. It then got to the point where I thought it was too late to call her, so I didn't. The guilt was heavy, and I did nothing about it. I thought of her often.

Not long after Rhys died, we ran into each other. Our daughters, who were born on the same day in the same hospital, had joined the same dancing class. We hugged and chatted as though no time had passed; then she said, "I'm so sorry I haven't been in touch, I just didn't know what to say." I told her the same thing, and we laughed about it.

If someone came to me today and said, "I'm sorry, Shan, I just didn't know what to say all those years ago," I'd be grateful for their bravery. We're all human, and the majority of us mean well. However, we sometimes have a tough time expressing our thoughts and feelings, and that's okay.

Embracing the new normal means navigating shifts in relationships with family and friends with sensitivity and openness. Bereaved parents might find that some relationships strengthen, while others falter or change. It's important for parents to communicate their needs and boundaries, while also being open to understanding how others are coping with the situation. Developing new social connections and finding supportive communities can help fill the gaps and foster a sense of belonging in this altered social landscape.

LIVING WITH LOSS

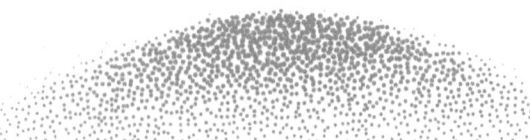

A Breath of Wisdom

Embracing the new normal is
about finding a balance between
honouring your child's memory
and continuing to live your life.

Consider how to best approach work,
family, and friendships to ensure you
can reclaim a level of normality.

Remember, we're all human, and
the majority of us mean well.

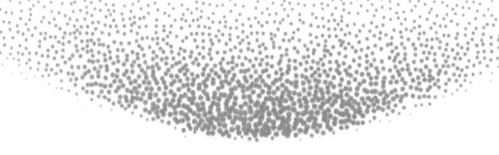

Chapter 14
Rediscovering Purpose

Rediscovering purpose after the death of a child involves a deeply personal journey of finding new meaning and direction in life. For many bereaved parents, this process begins with acknowledging their grief and giving themselves permission to feel and express their emotions. Allowing space for these feelings can create a foundation for healing.

Advocating for Change

As parents start to come to terms with their loss, they may find that their perspective on life shifts, revealing new insights and motivations. Embracing this change and being open to

You may be surprised to find you aren't the only one who is seeking change and to raise awareness. There's room for change, improvement, and advocacy everywhere you look.

exploring different avenues can lead to opportunities you never thought possible.

Parents may choose to become advocates for issues related to their child's death, such as raising awareness about a particular illness, safety issue, or social cause. By speaking out and working with organisations to promote change, they can channel their grief into meaningful action that benefits others and helps to bring about positive change in their communities.

Finding Purpose in Service and Support

Volunteering for local organisations or support groups can provide a sense of connection and purpose. By helping others who are in need, bereaved parents can find meaning in their actions. This involvement might include working with grief support groups, mentoring others who have experienced loss, or participating in community service projects.

Starting or joining a support group for other grieving parents or individuals can be a powerful way to find purpose. By sharing their experiences and offering support to others who are going through similar struggles, parents can create a sense of community and contribute to others' healing, which in turn can be deeply rewarding and fulfilling.

As mentioned in chapter five, a wonderful online support group is Bittersweet Parents. This is a respectful, closed group,  and approval is required to join. It brings together bereaved parents from across the world.
Bittersweet Parents Facebook group:
www.facebook.com/groups/bittersweetparents/

Other Sources of Purpose

One way bereaved parents can rediscover purpose is by engaging in activities or causes that resonate with their child's memory. By channelling their grief into positive actions, parents can create a meaningful legacy for their child, transforming their sorrow into a source of strength and motivation. You see it a lot – fundraisers for various charities to honour a child, memorial seats, and social events on anniversaries. Such endeavours not only offer a way to honour your child but also provide a sense of accomplishment and connection to something greater than yourself. We put our time and effort into the Rally for Rhys Foundation and the construction of the Halo Memorial at a local park.

I discuss the Halo Memorial further in chapter 20.

Additionally, bereaved parents may find purpose through personal growth and self-discovery. This could involve pursuing new hobbies, furthering education, or exploring creative outlets that they may not have considered before. Engaging in these activities can provide a sense of achievement and personal enrichment, helping to rebuild a sense of identity and purpose. It's essential for parents to remain patient with themselves throughout this journey, recognising that finding new meaning is a gradual process. By embracing their evolving interests and passions, bereaved parents can find new sources of joy and fulfilment, allowing them to navigate their grief while building a future that acknowledges both their loss and their potential for growth. Take it slowly and enjoy the experience.

Halo Memorial at Punchbowl Reserve.

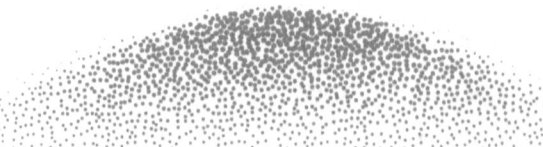

A Breath of Wisdom

Following the death of a child, it's important to rediscover your purpose.

Advocating for change and generating awareness around certain issues can be a great way to honour your child's memory.

Through action and purpose, grieving parents can turn their sorrow into a source of strength and motivation.

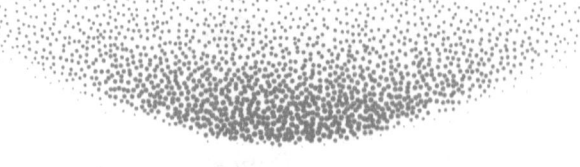

Chapter 15
The Negative Thoughts

Lifeline: 13 11 14

The loss of a child often triggers a cascade of painful emotions and troubling reflections that can significantly impact a bereaved parent's mental and emotional wellbeing. These negative thoughts are not only a natural part of the grieving process but also an intense manifestation of the deep-seated anguish and disorientation that accompanies such a profound loss. Understanding these thoughts and their implications can offer insight into the complex nature of grief and the paths towards healing and recovery.

Crippling Guilt and Insistent Self-Blame

One of the most pervasive negative thoughts that bereaved parents may experience is a profound sense of guilt. Parents might question their actions and decisions leading up to the child's death, wondering if there was something they could have done differently to prevent the loss. I remember having this conversation with my GP only days after Rhys died. I blamed his death on my parenting abilities. My supportive GP calmed me down and reassured me that my parenting ability had no role to play in the cause of Rhys's death. He reminded me how much Rhys was loved and that he was a lucky boy to have a mum like me. Sometimes, simple words of reassurance can mean so much when nothing in the world seems to make sense.

This self-blame can be exacerbated by the belief that you missed warning signs or didn't see it coming. The guilt can be compounded by societal pressures and expectations, where parents might feel judged or unsupported. Even if the child's death was due to factors beyond their control, such as illness or accident, the guilt can be overwhelming and persistent, leading to a harsh internal dialogue where they replay past moments in an attempt to find fault with themselves. This can be crippling and cruel for bereaved parents.

The Belief in Divine Retribution

Another common and deeply distressing thought is the belief that they are somehow being punished for something. Bereaved parents might struggle with the notion that their child's death is a form of divine retribution or cosmic justice. This belief can stem from a perceived failure or moral inadequacy, where parents feel they are being punished for past mistakes or sins. This type of thinking can further deepen their sense of isolation and despair, as it implies a personal fault or an imbalance that's beyond their ability to rectify.

A Sense of Hopelessness

The experience of hopelessness is another negative thought pattern that bereaved parents might grapple with. The profound loss of a child can lead to despair and a deep worry about the future. Parents may struggle with the belief that life will never be meaningful or enjoyable again. It's hard to see beyond the darkness and fog in the early days. The joy and dreams they had for their child are irreparably shattered. This hopelessness can affect their motivation to engage in daily activities, pursue goals, or maintain relationships, contributing to feelings of emotional numbness or depression. The future might seem bleak and uncertain, with the weight of the loss overshadowing any potential for recovery or new beginnings.

Neutralise the Negative Thoughts

The first step in addressing negative thoughts is to acknowledge, validate, and accept the emotions that come with them. It's important for bereaved parents to understand that experiencing intense feelings of guilt, anger, hopelessness, and isolation is a natural part of the grieving process. Recognising these emotions as natural responses to loss can help lessen their intensity and create a solid foundation for healing. I often needed to remind myself of this when I found myself spiralling into negative thoughts. Through the practice of mindfulness, I developed this skill, and it eventually became second nature to me.

As previously mentioned, professional counselling or therapy is a valuable resource for addressing and managing negative thoughts. A mental health professional, especially one specialising in grief and loss, can provide a safe and supportive environment to explore and process these thoughts. Therapy can help bereaved parents develop coping strategies, reframe negative thought patterns and work through feelings of guilt, anger, and hopelessness. These days, there are many different types of therapy consultants use to identify and challenge negative thought patterns, helping to replace them with more constructive and balanced perspectives. Take the time to choose a therapist who you feel comfortable with. Not everyone will be the right fit. It took me a few meetings with various therapists to realise this.

It's essential to give yourself permission to feel and express these emotions without self-judgement, recognising that they're a normal reaction to an extraordinary and painful situation.

Part of neutralising negative thoughts involves cultivating self-compassion. Self-compassion means treating yourself with the same kindness and understanding you would extend to a friend facing a similar situation. While it's easy to say, it's often much harder in practice! I know I can offer great advice to others but tend to be hard on myself in moments when my own advice would have been a kinder way to approach my feelings. I believe many of us experience this. Bereaved parents should cultivate self-compassion by recognising that they're doing their best in incredibly challenging circumstances. By challenging self-critical thoughts and replacing them with affirmations of their own strength and resilience, they can foster a more supportive internal dialogue.

Reframing involves shifting your perspective on negative thoughts to foster a hopeful outlook. If a bereaved parent is plagued by guilt, reframing might be as simple as recognising and accepting that grief is a complex and unpredictable process, even if that makes no sense to a grieving mind. It's natural to experience a range of emotions. Reframing negative thoughts can help reduce their impact and promote a more compassionate and constructive self-view, but it all takes time and practice in an overwhelming world.

I remember experiencing repetitive thoughts, often mentioning Rhys in nearly every sentence. It reached a point where it became noticeable, and Dean gently brought it to my attention.

I hadn't realised I was doing it, so his awareness helped me become more mindful of it. Naturally, we all think about Rhys every day, and in those early days he was always on our minds. However, I had developed a habit of repeating myself, and it was important for someone to point it out. I suppose this behaviour was tied to a temporary loss of cognitive skills and difficulty in controlling what I said, which was expected.

By being patient and gentle with yourself, you can navigate your grief with greater acceptance and resilience. Gradual healing also involves celebrating small steps forward.

Healing from the loss of a child is a gradual process that unfolds over time. It's important for parents to recognise that there's no 'right' way to grieve and no set timeline for healing.

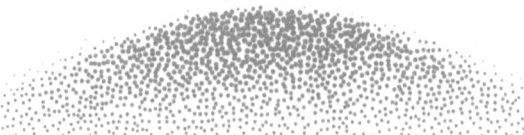

A Breath of Wisdom

The first step in addressing negative thoughts is to acknowledge, validate, and accept the emotions that come with them.

When experiencing negative thoughts, sometimes simple words of reassurance can make a world of difference.

Self-compassion is a crucial tool for breaking negative thought patterns.

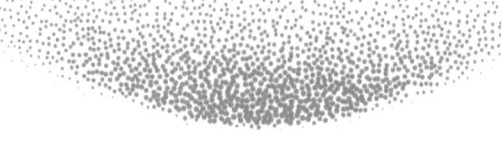

Part 6

Parenting Through Loss

Chapter 16
Supporting Siblings

Our daughter Amalie, now 14, has always been a fiercely independent girl. She rose to her feet and walked at 10 months, had a strong vocabulary for as long as I remember, and was the most empathetic toddler known to man. I remember one day in the car with then 4-year-old Ammi and the news came on the radio. Reports of war-torn Afghanistan. Ammi commented that it sounded like a scary movie and asked why everyone just can't be friends.

She was always the mother hen in her friendship group, making sure everyone was treated fairly, and she stood up for anyone who was being bullied. This often left her in a vulnerable position as a target for bullies. We had a lot of conversations around this topic.

When Ammi was in grade two, the mum of one of her classmates died of an illness. Ammi was 8 years old. She sat with this boy and told him about the pain in your tummy when someone you love dies, how it can hurt in your chest, deep in your heart.

Ammi and this boy had regular chats, and she made an impact on his life at such a devastating time.

When Rhys died, we were gifted some beautiful books, which Ammi fondly remembers reading. On Book Week dress-up day 2017, on the first anniversary of Rhys's death, Ammi dressed as the main character in *Brave as Can Be* by Jo Witek. It was significant and reflected who she was. She is a brave person who has faced so much adversity at such a young age.

The Protector Role

It's common for a grieving sibling to naturally slip into a protective role with their parents. Speaking with adult bereaved siblings who reflect back on the time their brother or sister died, they all reported doing this. Ammi was no different. We obviously didn't expect this from her, but she just took on the role. She matured overnight. It's an unfortunate reality for some children who lose siblings.

No Right Answers

Following Rhys's death, it was important for us to get Ammi back to school. The main reason was, we didn't want her to be around crying adults. We thought it would unsettle her even more. It's all such a blur. My brother Joel came with me, and we took Ammi back to school the day after Rhys died. Everyone was looking at me with looks of disbelief on their faces, and I remember thinking, *Oh no, what have I done?* But it was so important to get her back to her friends to smile and play. Ammi didn't end up staying on the day my brother and I took her in. She wanted to come home, and that was okay. I didn't know what the right decision was; I'm not sure there was one. We just did what we thought was right, and that's okay too. •

Some Welcome Love and Support

It was Book Week dress-up day, and Ammi wanted to show her friends her costume. Joel and I sat with the wonderful principal, Mrs Sally Milbourne. Sally provided so much love and support to us and Ammi for the remainder of her tenure at Norwood Primary School. Every time we visited the school, she would be right behind us, waiting for a cuddle. I spent so many days in Ammi's classroom, pinning children's artwork to the walls because I didn't know what to do with myself.

In the early days, Ammi's prep teacher Suze Chapple played such a huge role, and I look back with a safe and loving memory of how well I was supported during those agonisingly lonely days.

I remember promising Ammi I would come to school just so I would get out of bed. It must have been so comforting to Ammi too, having Mum there.

When Ammi returned to school, because the school had time to inform all parents that Rhys had died and sought their permission to notify the children, the most beautiful moment occurred in the classroom. Suze Chapple sat all the children, all aged 5 and 6, on the mat and told them Ammi's little brother had died. She explained that Ammi would be feeling sad for a while and asked them what they could do to make her feel better. They started raising their little hands, suggesting all the things they could do to make Ammi feel happy.

"Give her a cuddle."

"Smile at her if she looks sad."

"Play fun games with her."

I'll never forget this moment for as long as I live. What a beautiful gesture of love and support to offer such a young child. Thanks, Suze, we love you.

The students also made a book for Amalie over the coming week for her to refer to when she felt sad to remind her how loved and supported she was.

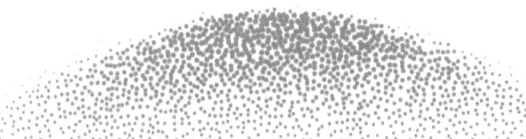

A Breath of Wisdom

Bereaved siblings may adopt a protector role towards their parents.

When deciding how to best support a bereaved sibling, sometimes there are no right answers. Everyone's journey and experience are different.

A supportive school environment is key to easing the transition back to relative normalcy.

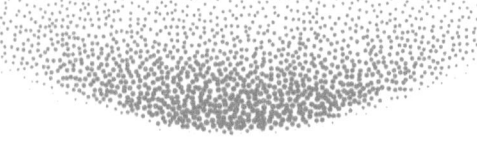

Chapter 17
Returning to School, Restoring Normalcy

The return to school after the death of a sibling can be one of the most daunting transitions for bereaved families. The place that once felt safe and familiar can suddenly become a source of distress. All eyes on you, word spreads quickly through school communities, especially with something as tragic as the loss of a child. Trauma and panic can make people do strange things. This chapter explores the various challenges families may face during this sensitive period.

The Challenges of Returning to School

For a bereaved sibling, the classroom can become a reminder of their loss. The presence of classmates, teachers, and even routines may trigger intense emotions. Families often report that the surviving child struggles to concentrate. Grief can cloud cognitive functions, making it difficult to focus on lessons, assignments, or discussions. Sudden outbursts or emotional surges can result in tears or anger, which can manifest unexpectedly in the classroom. Teachers and peers might struggle to understand these reactions, leading to further isolation.

The bereaved sibling might choose to isolate themselves from friends, feeling different or disconnected from their peers. This withdrawal can deepen feelings of loneliness and abandonment. Returning to school often means facing peers who may not know how to respond to the loss. This can lead to several challenging scenarios, including classmates who may be unaware of the sibling's death or may express discomfort at discussing it. Phrases like, "Aren't you over it by now?" and other hurtful comments may arise as peers attempt to 'try to fix' the bereaved sibling. Remarks like, "At least you have your other siblings" can feel dismissive of the unique bond that has been lost.

The response from teachers and school staff can significantly impact a bereaved sibling's experience. Many educators may lack grief support training, which can lead to misunderstanding or mishandling of the sibling's emotional needs. This may result in punitive measures for behaviours that stem from grief rather than misbehaviour. It's important for a bereaved parent to find out which teachers are best to approach to support their child, even if it's someone they can go to during the day if they need someone to talk to. Without established support systems, such as counselling or peer support groups, the school may fall short in providing the emotional support the bereaved sibling needs.

Educators may also have expectations for the sibling to return to their previous academic performance and social behaviours, creating pressure that can be overwhelming. Academic performance can pause or even go backwards after such a traumatic experience. Children need to be represented to find support in the school system if it's not offered upfront.

The impact of grief extends beyond the bereaved sibling and can alter family dynamics, complicating the school transition. Parents may be preoccupied with their own grief, leaving the surviving sibling feeling neglected or unsupported. This lack of attention can exacerbate feelings of loneliness. Other siblings may feel compelled to take on additional responsibilities or may struggle with their own grief, further complicating the atmosphere at home and impacting their emotional wellbeing. With parents and caregivers grappling with their own emotions, the bereaved sibling may receive inconsistent support, leading to confusion and instability in their emotional state.

Easing the Transition

Despite the challenges, there are ways families can prepare for and ease into the transition back to school. Families can work with school staff before the sibling returns to establish a supportive environment. This might involve creating a plan that includes check-ins with teachers and access to counselling resources.

Preparing the surviving sibling to communicate with classmates about their loss can help ease feelings of isolation. Families can role-play potential conversations, helping the sibling express their feelings in a way that feels comfortable.

Establishing a consistent daily routine can provide a sense of normalcy and stability in the face of chaos, helping the bereaved sibling regain a foothold in their school life.

The return to school after the death of a sibling is fraught with challenges, affecting not just the bereaved child but the entire family. By understanding these potential pitfalls and proactively addressing them, families can create a supportive environment. With compassion and patience, it is possible to foster resilience and healing.

Advice from a School Social Worker

I sat and spoke with a dear friend of mine, Laura, an experienced social worker at a local high school. I asked her what support

Acknowledging that emotional responses may fluctuate can help families set realistic expectations for the sibling's behaviour and academic performance during this transition.

generally looks like for school-aged, bereaved siblings within our state. The following paragraphs are her words.

What to Expect from the School

First, you could expect the school to rally together to support not only the student but also the student's family. My advice would be to contact the school at the earliest convenience. Initial contact would be to discuss attendance and while it's important for the student to return to school for some normality and routine, conversations within the school need to have taken place to ensure the young person is supported.

Depending on the size of the school and the relationships built, the school community will most likely be made aware that the family has suffered the loss of their child/sibling, but this can also happen naturally at the family's discretion, with confidentiality where necessary and respect. In my experience, maybe a few core staff will be made aware of what has happened. That would be the class teacher, the principal, and then maybe some senior staff, depending on the student's and family's needs.

They would certainly be keeping an extra close eye on the young person, and adjustments might be made in the classroom where appropriate. The school will be aware that a young person who has experienced trauma or distress may be sitting outside of their window of tolerance. Academic achievements might take a back seat for a little while. The real focus would be on social emotional learning, which is a big focus in schools.

I think it's important to reiterate that, depending on circumstances, the sooner the young person returns to school, the better. Routine is so important, and getting back into the swing of normality can be helpful on their journey. Not just for the children in the family, but for the parents as well.

Open Communication is Key

Keeping communication open with the school, whether it be primary school or high school, is important.

With high school, you've got a lot of different subject teachers to deal with. Generally, you'd speak to a support teacher or the principal, and they would inform all relevant teaching staff that the student has suffered a significant loss. No specific details should be shared; however, the family should be given the opportunity to share details if they wish. Teaching staff will be instructed to keep an extra eye on this student and make sure they're okay. Any alarm bells, and they should let a key contact person know, for example, the assistant principal for the grade. It should be the same person who is liaising with the parents because you don't need too many people involved, ideally just one person reporting back home.

I think with teenagers, it's important they can go to a teacher they have a good relationship with and can talk to openly. Same with primary school – they can self-refer through a support staff member, or they can speak to a teacher, asking to speak to someone privately and, therefore, accessing counselling within school. If, having experienced quite complex grief, the student needs additional support, external referrals can be arranged. Families would be contacted for consent first.

A School-Based Strategy

An issue you might have with an adolescent is wagging school or non-attendance. It's harder to keep tabs on teenagers compared to primary school children, who you're dropping off and picking up on a regular basis. Generally, if a student doesn't show, the school will let the parents know immediately as part of their attendance procedures.

Wagging is about avoidance, and, from my experience, teens can sometimes turn to more risky behaviours as a way of coping. It's worth noting that this can be normal behaviour and, I suppose, try not to be alarmed. However, you obviously don't want it to persist for too long.

Giving the child a clear plan can help minimise harmful coping strategies. For example, if the student is in class and starts to feel distressed, options may include the school providing a leave pass with specific instructions. They may be instructed to go to a designated location (for example, the principal's office or library) to do an activity that will help them feel more comfortable in that moment (for example, reading, journalling, music, mindfulness activities). If the student needs to stay in class, they may have a journal in their desk that they could take 5 minutes to write in. They may just need fresh air and the option to go for a walk. I know that students sometimes have a favourite teacher and subject, so they could have the option to join that class, no questions asked. Going to the grade leader's office is another good one. Essentially, you're trying to help them regulate while only being out of class for a short time. They shouldn't miss out on too much learning, but, at the same time, you're prioritising their social and emotional wellbeing over the academic requirements for a little while.

The chosen option needs to be practical and prearranged, and all parties involved must be aware of the plan. It keeps the child within the safety of the school grounds with people around them to assist. This should be led by the school. Families shouldn't have to instigate this.

The Right Support

In my experience, children in primary school and even pre-kinder tend to express their distress by either externalising or internalising their feelings (shutting down). The strategy to support the student would be something orchestrated by their teacher, and there would be a definitive pathway forward. Then a plan would be put in place for how to re-engage or regulate that young person when they're distressed. This could involve going into the playground, or it might be reading a story. Some primary schools now have mindfulness rooms. I've been teaching in mindfulness rooms recently where rules exist such as quiet space or no stimulation. It's a great space, and, if possible, the school may incorporate that environment into a young person's timetable. If the child returns to school and only needs a bit of additional support, some schools have therapy dogs. All great ideas.

Another reassurance for families is that schools aren't just focusing on that bereaved sibling and family members, but also on the friendship groups around the sibling. I think some families do worry about the other people and other families that are affected. Just to reassure you, those families would also be looked after by the school.

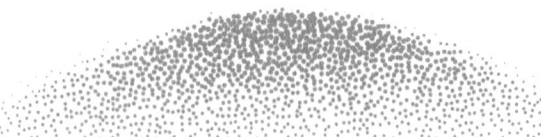

A Breath of Wisdom

Before a bereaved sibling returns to school, it's important that the parents work with staff to create a plan and ensure a smooth transition.

Ongoing, open communication is key, ideally with one specific contact within the school.

Children, especially teens, can turn to risky behaviour as a way to cope. While this is normal, it shouldn't be allowed to persist for too long.

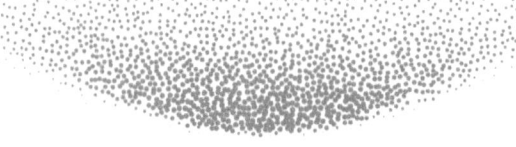

Chapter 18
Grief Regression

The echoes of loss resonate differently in each family, shaping the emotional landscape in unexpected ways. Among these dynamics, the experience of bereaved siblings can be particularly profound and complex. I learnt how childhood trauma and grief evolve as children age. We were advised not to force any intervention, just to let Ammi drive her feelings and speak to us freely about how she was feeling. We've always spoken openly and often about Rhys in our family and home, mostly about memories, mannerisms, and so on. Ammi loves talking about Rhys and looking at photos of him.

Unlike parents, who often find ways to navigate the acute pain of losing a child, siblings can find themselves caught in a unique web of emotions: love, jealousy, guilt, and sometimes a regression into behaviours long left behind.

Upon Rhys's passing, his absence created a void that shifted Ammi's identity and sense of self, leading to grief regression.

From the moment Rhys entered the world, a bond like no other formed between him and Ammi – a relationship characterised by shared experiences, mutual understanding, sometimes fierce rivalry but also an immense love for each other.

Grief regression refers to the re-emergence of earlier developmental behaviours as individuals struggle to cope with overwhelming loss. For bereaved siblings, this can manifest in various ways.

Childlike behaviours. In the wake of loss, an older sibling may begin to exhibit behaviours typical of younger children, such as seeking comfort items (like stuffed animals or blankets) or wanting to be treated more like a child. This regression serves as a coping mechanism, allowing the sibling to escape the harsh realities of adulthood. Ammi started talking like a baby and asked for help with things like tying shoes, eating dinner, and brushing her teeth.

Emotional outbursts. Intense emotions, including anger, sadness, and confusion, can be more frequent, leading to tantrums or aggressive behaviour, reminiscent of earlier developmental stages when emotions were less regulated. Conversely, some siblings may retreat into themselves, preferring solitude over social interaction. This regression into introversion can be a way to cope with feelings of inadequacy as they grapple with the fear that they can't live up to the memory of their lost sibling.

Changes in interests. A bereaved sibling might abandon hobbies and interests they once loved, reverting to activities that remind them of their lost sibling. This shift can be a way of holding on to the past, even as they struggle to find joy in the present.

The Role of Family Dynamics

Family responses to the death of a sibling can further complicate the grieving process. Parents may be so consumed by their own grief that they inadvertently overlook the needs of the surviving child. In such cases, the bereaved sibling may feel invisible, intensifying feelings of abandonment and leading to more pronounced regressive behaviours.

Conversely, some parents might try to 'fill the void' left by the deceased child, placing unrealistic expectations on the surviving sibling to take on new roles within the family. This can create immense pressure, often resulting in rebellion or regression as the sibling struggles against these new demands. I recall Ammi taking on the role of parenting us, wanting to care for us and being our protector.

Understanding grief regression in bereaved siblings is crucial for families navigating this challenging terrain. To help support the surviving sibling, let them know that it's normal to experience a range of emotions, including those that may seem contradictory or difficult to understand. Validate their grief and remind them that regression is a common response.

Ammi has experienced certain worries in her life that can arise in a bereaved sibling. Worrying that she is going to die or that we (Dean, Elijah, and I) are going to die, visualising accidents happening and other similar trauma responses. Some of these worries are only recent, which shows how her grief and trauma have evolved as she has come to realise the enormity of what happened to her and our family. We support her always, but especially during these times, and seek specialist assistance when required.

The journey of grief is rarely linear, and, for bereaved siblings, it's often marked by regression into past behaviours and emotional struggles. By fostering understanding, open communication, and supportive environments, families can help navigate the complex terrain of grief. The love between siblings is a bond that endures beyond death, and through compassion and support, surviving siblings can find ways to honour their lost loved ones while carving their own paths forward.

We're so proud of Ammi. She has achieved a lot in her 14 years and continues to do her best. She's a healthy, beautiful girl, wise beyond her years, with the emotional strength of a saint. She's a force to be reckoned with on the hockey field and loves spending time with her friends. It's important we give her the life she deserves and for her to not feel different from other kids but to embrace her resilience and strength. Rhys will always be a big part of her life.

While it's important to acknowledge regression, encouraging independence and personal growth can help the sibling redefine their identity outside of their sibling's shadow.

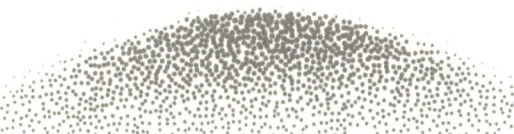

A Breath of Wisdom

Bereaved siblings can experience grief regression – that is, the re-emergence of earlier developmental behaviours, such as exhibiting childlike behaviours and emotional outbursts.

The family's response to the death of a sibling can influence the surviving sibling's reaction and potential to experience grief regression.

When navigating the complex terrain of grief, fostering understanding, open communication, and supportive environments is crucial.

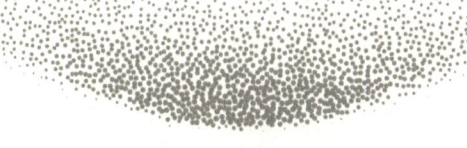

Part 7

Legacy

Chapter 19

Projects and Activities in Rhys's Memory

About 6 months after Rhys passed away, my sister-in-law Anna approached me with a heartfelt idea. She wanted to honour Rhys's memory, and being an incredible cook with her own cake decorating business, it was natural for her to suggest a high tea. We sat down together and started to sketch out a rough plan to invite family and friends to gather, share memories of Rhys, and enjoy delicious cakes. If you know me well, you understand that I tend to dive in headfirst – even the smallest spark of an idea can quickly grow into something monumental after just a short conversation.

In 2018, we organised the Rally for Rhys Bittersweet High Tea in collaboration with Lisa Bird, the founder of Bittersweet Parents. We gathered with 300 of our closest friends and raised $30,000 to install a memorial Halo in Punchbowl Reserve, Launceston.

Thus, the Rally for Rhys
Foundation was born,
a charitable fund created
in Rhys's memory to
support bereaved families,
especially focusing on
bereaved siblings.

The event featured a beautiful high tea with live music, a lively auction, and a candlelit tribute to the many children remembered by the members of the Bittersweet Parents Facebook group. We also included a creators' market and provided a quiet space where qualified social workers were available to those in need of support. The auction items were generously donated by wonderful individuals, and one of the final items – a plaque awarded to "the most generous person in the room" with no tangible prize – raised an astonishing $1,500 for the Rally for Rhys Foundation. It was a heartwarming moment, watching numerous hands raise to bid for nothing but the title of pure generosity.

The day was unforgettable, and we were honoured to be finalists and win awards for Halo, which has since become a sacred place for bereaved families to visit. It's also a popular spot for weddings, leavers' dinners, and family gatherings. I love receiving photos of Halo, witnessing it be part of cherished memories for others.

Every year since then, I've brought up the idea of organising another event, only to be reminded by my family of the countless hours we all dedicated to the high tea. They suggest that maybe "down the track" we might consider it again. I truly appreciate how my family keeps me grounded!

Rally for Rhys Market Cake Stalls

Leading up to the high tea, my wonderful friend proposed a cake stall at a local market, where we raised over $2,000. This support was crucial in getting Rally for Rhys off the ground and securing deposits for the event. The sheer number of people who volunteered their time and ingredients was incredible. It really showcased the generosity of our community, and I was truly amazed.

On another occasion, family and friends of family dedicated time to baking, stitching, and raising more funds for Rally for Rhys. Hearts were poured into preparing for another stall at the Swansea Fair in the town where Dean's parents live.

Countless hours were spent creating beautiful, meaningful items to sell. From delicious cakes to unique handmade crafts, every contribution was aimed at providing comfort and support to families and siblings.

Rally for Rhys Evandale Market stall.

Halo Launch Event

One year to the day after the high tea, in May 2019, we celebrated the unveiling of Halo at Punchbowl Reserve in Launceston. The local council granted us permission to set up marquees and invite food vans to the event, a first for the reserve. With live music, burgers, and sunshine, it turned into a truly special day, allowing us to showcase Halo in all her glory and demonstrate to the community what their contributions had made possible.

Love Your Sister/Rally for Rhys Fundie

Samuel Johnson OAM is the co-founder of Love Your Sister, an Australian charity dedicated to funding the nation's brightest and most innovative medical researchers and clinicians. Their mission is to provide all cancer patients with precision treatments and to enhance access to new techniques and integrated data for medical professionals.

In September 2019, Sam and Love Your Sister embarked on a nationwide journey to rally Australians as 'villagers' to support their cause. When they reached Tasmania, they encouraged locals to host events called 'fundies'. Naturally, I volunteered (along with my ever-supportive family and friends) and managed to coordinate an event at our local PCYC (in approximately 3 days!) for over 150 people to meet Sam and sign up for this worthy cause.

That day, Sam declared it one of his biggest sign-up events to date, with more than 50 attendees committing to donate monthly to Love Your Sister. It was an incredible day for everyone touched by cancer as we united to take a stand against the disease.

Sam arrived with his Gold Logie in one hand and his *Dancing with the Stars* trophy in the other, creating a wonderful atmosphere for the local community. We enjoyed a cheerleading performance, played giant-sized board games, and placed ribbons on a memorial wall in honour of those we'd lost to cancer.

Sam also spoke with Ammi about the pain of losing a sibling. Since then, Ammi has organised fundraisers at her school for Sam and Love Your Sister. He has sent her thank-you videos, called me with ideas, and even included little love notes with our purchases from the Love Your Sister store. It's a beautiful connection, and Ammi is committed to supporting this charity for the rest of her life, which I know she will follow through on. We truly love Love Your Sister.

Samuel Johnson from Love Your Sister inspiring the crowd at our collaborative fundraising event.

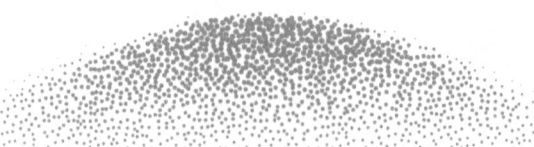

A Breath of Wisdom

Special projects and events are a great way to honour your child's memory.

Collaborating with other groups or organisations can be beneficial.

The generosity of others
is truly amazing.

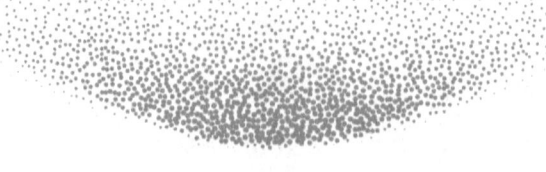

Chapter 20
Giving Back and Helping Others

In the wake of Rhys's passing, grief enveloped me, leaving me to navigate the world as a shadow of my former self. But amid the darkness, there was a definitive glimmer of light – a way to honour Rhys's memory by giving back and supporting others who were also navigating the painful journey of loss. I was driven a lot by the fear of what the alternative was. I was searching for my purpose, and it honestly didn't take long to find it.

I created a vision – to live in a world where newly bereaved parents receive global support, feel less isolated, and unite to save lives and eradicate the stigma surrounding child loss.

The Initial Spark

It all stemmed from the conversation I had with my sister-in-law Anna before the birth of the Rally for Rhys Foundation, along with becoming part of a network of other bereaved parents through Bittersweet Parents and finding a platform to share our story.

Hearing others speak about their own experiences created a sense of connection that made me feel less isolated. It was during those conversations that I realised I wasn't alone and that I felt better by speaking about child loss and being able to speak Rhys's name. There were others like me, carrying the heavy burden of loss, seeking solace and understanding. I felt compelled to do something to help others who were struggling.

Creating a Legacy

As stated, and inspired by our personal experience, we created the Rally for Rhys Foundation. It was a tangible way to give back, allowing me to support other families facing similar tragedies. The fundraising events and reaching out to the community for support removed the stigma associated with child loss, all while we connected and supported each other.

Supporting Other Bereaved Parents

One of the most profound aspects of giving back was the relationships I built with other bereaved parents. We listened to one another's stories, offered comfort, and found strength in shared understanding. I remember one mother whose pain mirrored my own. Our boys died at the same age, within months of each other and both suddenly in their sleep as the result of a febrile convulsion. She lives on the other side of the world, but distance was no barrier, and we connected instantly. As we shared our journeys, we both held a glimmer of hope when we realised we weren't alone. Supporting each other became a powerful reminder of our resilience.

Finding Hope in Helping Others

Through my journey of giving back, I discovered a renewed sense of hope. Helping others navigate their grief became a source of healing for me.

Giving back became more than just a way to honour Rhys; it transformed into a lifeline for my own healing. In sharing my story and supporting others, I found purpose where I once felt lost. It's a journey that continues to evolve, reminding me that even in the depths of grief, there is light to be found in connection and community.

Each smile, each thank you from a parent who felt seen and understood reaffirmed that Rhys's legacy was alive and well in the hearts of others.

As bereaved parents, we often search for meaning in our loss. For me, the path to finding purpose lay in giving back. By extending compassion to others, I discovered the profound healing that comes from shared experiences. If you find yourself on a similar journey, I encourage you to reach out, connect, and give back. You may just find that in supporting others, you also begin to heal.

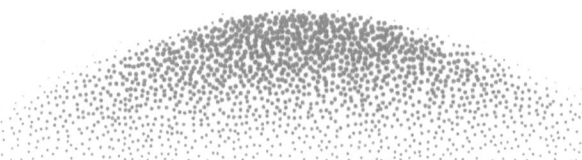

A Breath of Wisdom

Giving back can be incredibly healing.

Through supporting others, you build lifelong relationships.

If you're yet to find your purpose, don't stop looking – it's out there, waiting to be discovered.

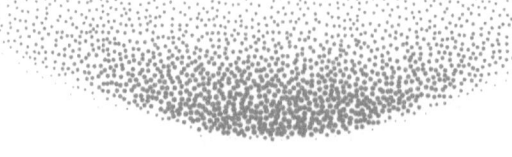

Chapter 21

My 'Why'

In the quiet moments, when the world feels still and the weight of grief sits heavy on my heart, I often find myself reflecting on my 'why'. Why do I wake up each day and strive to make a difference in the lives of others? It would be easier to feel sorry for myself and hide under a rock. I'm not going to pretend that every day I need to remind myself why I'm doing this and what I'm grateful for. It's an active choice. Why do I pour my energy into honouring Rhys's memory? The answer lies in the legacy I wish to leave behind – a legacy that embodies love, resilience, and hope. Without love, resilience, and hope, I wouldn't be here today to tell our story.

Understanding My Why

Each tear shed, each moment of heartache, and each outburst of raw anger for my situation became a catalyst for action. In those early days, I often felt overwhelmed by the weight of my grief. It was as if I was carrying a heavy stone in my chest, making it difficult to breathe. As I worked my way through the haze of grief, I started to understand that these powerful emotions could be redirected into something meaningful. It was a journey I needed to undertake, a path that would lead me towards a destination where I could make a difference and honour Rhys.

Those tears became a release, a way to acknowledge that my grief wasn't just an end, but a powerful reminder of the life that once filled my world with joy. With each tear, I found myself more committed to ensuring that Rhys's life – however brief – would leave a lasting mark on this world. I couldn't change what had happened, but I could influence how others perceived grief, remove the stigma associated with child loss, and highlight how we could support one another.

My anger, too, became fuel for change. I felt rage at the injustice of losing my child, at the world that continued to spin while my heart was shattered. But in those moments of fury, I also found clarity. That anger pushed me to take action, to fight against the silence and stigma surrounding child loss. I realised that I could transform my anguish into a powerful voice, advocating for other bereaved families who might feel as isolated as I once did.

When I cried, I wasn't just expressing my pain; I was honouring the depth of my love.

In those moments,
I was reminded that
love has no boundaries,
not even in death.

Through this process, I began to understand that Rhys's spirit could continue to live on through the love and kindness I extended to others. Each time I reached out to support another grieving parent, each moment I shared my story, each moment I spoke Rhys's name, I felt his presence guiding me.

I listened to other parents share their stories of loss. Their pain echoed my own, creating a bond that transcended words.

By offering empathy and understanding to others, feeling their pain, I was keeping Rhys's memory alive in a way that mattered.

As I organised community events and fundraisers, each act of kindness became a tribute to Rhys. I envisioned the legacy I wanted to build – not just for myself, but for him too. I wanted to create a space where families could come together, share their stories, and find hope amid their grief. My tears weren't wasted; they transformed into a source of strength that propelled me to act.

With every connection I made and every life I touched, I felt a profound sense of purpose. I began to understand that while Rhys may no longer be here physically, his spirit could thrive through the love I shared. I dedicated myself to making a difference, whether through supporting bereaved families, advocating for awareness, or simply offering a comforting presence to someone in need.

In this journey of grief, I discovered that our loved ones never truly leave us. They live on in the stories we share, the kindness we show, and the lives we touch. Each tear, each moment of heartache, and each surge of anger became the foundation for a legacy built on love, reminding me that I could extend the compassion Rhys inspired within me to others. Through this work, I realised that healing is a collective journey, and by carrying his spirit with me, I could help illuminate the path for others walking through their own darkness.

The Power of Legacy

Leaving a legacy is about more than just memories; it's also about impact. I wanted to create something that would carry our story forward, something that would resonate with others facing similar pain. This realisation ignited a fire within me, a determination to make a difference in the lives of bereaved families.

I started to think about how I could honour Rhys's memory in a way that would help others navigate their grief. This longing to connect and support became the foundation of my 'why'. I envisioned a world where families like mine would find comfort, understanding, and resources in their darkest hours. A world where bereaved parents receive global support, feel less isolated, and unite to save lives and eradicate the stigma surrounding child loss.

Creating a Supportive Community

Driven by my desire to help, I began reaching out to other bereaved parents. I became a part of support groups where we shared our stories or photos on days when there were no words. We shared our pain, and we shared our hope. I found solace in knowing that we weren't alone; our shared experiences forged bonds that transcended words.

 **Bittersweet Parents Facebook group:** www.facebook.com/groups/bittersweetparents/

Advocating for Awareness and Change

As my journey continues, I endeavour to advocate and raise awareness around child loss. I want to ensure that other families don't have to endure the isolation we faced. With this book tucked under my arm, I endeavour to educate and break the stigma surrounding child loss. My advocacy is still in its early stages, but I envision changes in school curricula to formalise a process that helps bereaved siblings reintegrate into the education system after losing a brother or sister. I also want to work on improving the ways hospital staff offer comfort to grieving families, tailored to the age of the child lost.

I aspire to travel and learn from different cultures about their grieving practices, exploring how we might enhance our

By illuminating these experiences, I aim to create a legacy that fosters compassion and understanding for those navigating their grief.

approach to grief in Western society. My goal is to save lives by offering support when it's truly needed, rather than waiting until it's too late.

Through my advocacy, I've shared my story publicly and will continue to do so, exposing the vulnerability of my pain. It's raw and real. It's not staged. I want others to see that while loss is profoundly difficult, it can also bring us together in our shared humanity.

Honouring Rhys's Memory

I discovered that creating a tangible legacy was vital to my healing process. Even though we've founded the Rally for Rhys Foundation, our journey has only just begun. I envision Rally for Rhys evolving into a comprehensive support system, offering counselling services, financial assistance, and more meaningful community events. This foundation is poised to become a beacon of hope for many, providing the resources I wished I had when I first faced this unimaginable journey.

Each event we organise serves as a celebration of life, honouring not just Rhys but every child taken too soon. The laughter and love shared at these gatherings remind me that joy can coexist with grief. It's a beautiful way to extend support to others in their time of need.

The Ongoing Journey

My 'why' has become a guiding light, illuminating the path forward as I navigate my grief. Each act of kindness, each connection made brings me closer to fulfilling the legacy I aspire to leave. I understand now that while Rhys may not be here physically, his presence lives on through the love I share and the impact I make.

I continue to learn and grow through this journey. The legacy I aim to leave is one of love, resilience, and hope.

Download your own Rhys Random Act of Kindness cards.
rallyforrhys.com.au/wp-content/uploads/2018/01/RAOK_Rhys_A4x4.pdf

Our vision is a world where newly bereaved parents receive global support, feel less isolated, and unite to save lives and eradicate the stigma surrounding child loss.

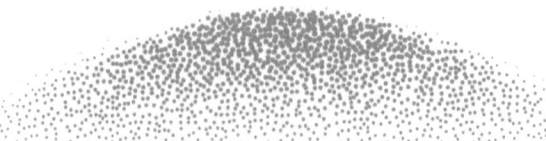

A Breath of Wisdom

Heartache and anger can be
fuel for action and change.

Our loved ones live on through us,
through our words and our actions.

Creating a legacy not only helps
you heal, but also helps others.

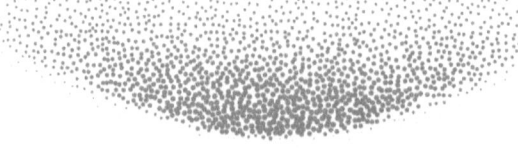

Part 8

The Journey Continues

Chapter 22

Reflections on the Journey

One of the most surprising aspects of my journey was the gradual return of joy. I remember the first time I laughed after Rhys died; it felt foreign yet liberating. I realised that embracing joy didn't diminish my love for Rhys. I began to seek out moments of happiness – watching a sunset, enjoying a good meal, or spending time with loved ones. These moments became essential reminders that life still held beauty and that it was okay to feel happiness again.

Cultivating Hope for the Future

As I emerged from the abyss, I began to cultivate hope for the future. It was a slow process, but I started to envision a life that, while different, could still be fulfilling. Rhys would always be a part of my story, shaping who I am and how I interact with the world. I learnt to embrace the uncertainty of life, understanding that it could still be rich with experiences.

This new-found hope gave me the courage to set goals, both small and large. I wanted to travel, to explore new places, to create memories. With each step I took, I felt a sense of empowerment. I wasn't defined by my loss; I was defined by my resilience and my ability to love deeply.

A New Chapter

Reflecting on my journey as a bereaved parent, I can see the profound transformation that has taken place within me. I have emerged from the shadows of grief with a renewed sense of purpose and connection. I carry Rhys's memory with me as a source of strength, allowing it to guide me towards healing and hope.

While the pain of loss will always be a part of my life, I've learnt to integrate it into my identity. I'm not just a bereaved parent; I'm a survivor, a person who has navigated the depths of sorrow and emerged with a heart that's still capable of love. My journey is ongoing, and I know there will be challenges ahead. But I'm armed with the understanding that healing is possible, that joy can coexist with grief, and that transformation can emerge from the most profound pain.

I will continue to honour Rhys by living fully, by cherishing every moment, and by embracing the lessons this journey has taught me.

In this new chapter of my life, I continue to seek beauty, connection, and purpose.

Deciding to Have Another Child

Reflecting on the moment Dean and I decided to have another child after Rhys's passing, I remember feeling incredibly torn and hurt. It's hard to articulate. I wished someone else could have made that decision for us; I didn't want to face the question of whether having another child was a good idea. What ultimately eased that burden was realising I was lucky enough to have a choice, which began to make sense for us. Many others don't have that luxury. The loss of a child takes many forms, including the heartbreak of a parent losing their only adult child. Their sense of parenthood can vanish in an instant, and they may not have the option to have another child, which deeply saddens me.

Once we made the decision to expand our family, I became pregnant within a few months, filling our household with a renewed focus and bubbling excitement. I knew another child wouldn't replace Rhys. My unborn child would be my third. Feeling fortunate to be in a position to welcome another child, it turned out to be the most healing choice we could have made. When we found out we were having another red-headed boy, it was a surprising and somewhat overwhelming moment! We're so grateful for Elijah Rhys. He has brought a lightness to our lives and has made our family of five feel complete again. He truly is a ray of sunshine.

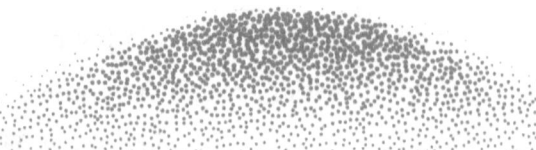

A Breath of Wisdom

Over time, the ability to
experience joy does return, and
joy and grief can coexist.

Loss doesn't define us. Instead, we're
defined by our positive traits, such as
resilience and the ability to love deeply.

The journey is ongoing.

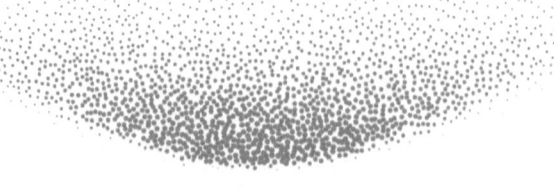

Chapter 23

Finding Purpose and Meaning

In the aftermath of losing a child, it may seem impossible to find purpose or meaning again. Yet, many have discovered that while grief is a heavy burden to carry, it can also pave the way to a deeper understanding of life and a renewed sense of purpose.

Grief – a Complex Journey

As previously noted, grief isn't a straightforward journey; it can surprise you, and the intensity of that grief can feel overwhelming, affecting you from day to day and even moment to moment. Understanding the complexities of grief is crucial to beginning the healing journey.

After losing a child, you will experience a range of emotions: shock, anger, guilt, and profound sadness. These feelings can manifest in various ways: sleepless nights, difficulty concentrating, or a sense of isolation. No one should walk this path alone. Finding support is crucial to healing. At the back of the book, I've listed some support groups and resources, which are a great place to start for bereaved parents, even just for a chat. Sharing your experience with those who understand can reduce feelings of isolation.

Let loved ones know how they can support you. Sometimes, simply having someone listen can be incredibly comforting. Don't shy away from asking for help when you need it.

As you navigate through grief, it may feel as though joy is permanently out of reach. Try by starting small. Engage in activities that once brought you joy, even if they seem trivial. Maybe this is gardening, reading, or taking a walk. Allowing yourself these moments can gradually help you reconnect with happiness. Meditation, yoga, or simple breathing exercises can offer clarity as you process your feelings. Laughter may feel foreign after a loss, but it's essential for healing. Surround yourself with people who uplift you and engage in activities that make you smile, even if only for a moment. You'll thank yourself for allowing some space to breathe and relax.

The Path to Purpose

The loss of a child may lead you to reassess your life's purpose. While the journey is undoubtedly painful, it can also open up new avenues for growth. Re-evaluating your values and reflecting on what truly matters is important. Has your perspective shifted? Take time to identify your core values and how they may guide you moving forward. If this makes no sense now, time will help to bring clarity. Be kind to yourself. Stepping outside your comfort zone can lead to unexpected joy and fulfilment.

Remember that your child's love and spirit can guide you. Reflect on the qualities that defined them and find ways to embody those traits in your life. Consider how you can create a legacy in your child's name. If it seems too overwhelming, ask friends who are creative. They may think of an idea that surprises you and ignites a profound feeling of pride for your child. It could also be something like advocating for issues or illness that had an effect on you or your child. There's no greater force than a bereaved mother or father defending their child. Use your experience to connect with others. Sharing your story can help others who are suffering.

Finding purpose after the loss of a child is a journey filled with ups and downs. Embrace the complexities of your emotions and give yourself permission to heal at your own pace. Accept that grief will always be a part of your life, but it doesn't have to define you. Acknowledge even the smallest steps you take towards healing. Celebrate your progress, no matter how minor it may seem. Each step is a testament to your strength. While it may feel impossible at times, allow yourself to envision a future filled with possibility. It may not seem like it now, but you can build a life rich with meaning, even after profound loss.

Finding purpose and meaning after the loss of a child is an ongoing process that requires time, patience, and love. By seeking support, rediscovering joy, and embracing the journey ahead, you can navigate this path towards healing. Remember, you're not alone; countless others have walked this road and emerged stronger, carrying their children with them in their hearts. Your journey may be uniquely yours, but the love you shared is eternal.

Your child's memory will always be a part of you and will shape your identity and purpose in profound ways.

ONE BREATH AT A TIME

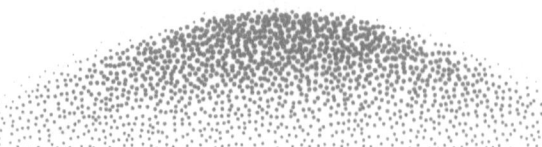

A Breath of Wisdom

Grief is a complex journey,
with many ups and downs.

Seek support from others
when you're ready.

Rediscovering purpose and meaning
is an important part of the journey.

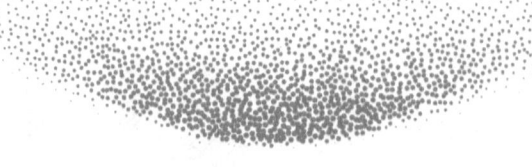

Chapter 24

Moving Forward with Grief

Living with loss doesn't mean leaving your grief behind; rather, it involves finding a way to move forward while carrying it with you. It's about acknowledging that grief is a part of your journey, not just a moment to be overcome. As you navigate your daily life, you learn to integrate loss into your new reality.

This process doesn't imply forgetting or minimising your feelings, but instead it invites you to embrace them as a testament to a deep love for your child. It's okay to feel sadness, anger, or confusion as you adjust. Those emotions can coexist with joy and happiness.

Moving forward might mean creating new traditions or finding ways to keep your child's memory alive in your heart and mind. It can also involve seeking support from others who understand, sharing stories, or even finding comfort in your own company. It's about redefining your relationship with your grief. Instead of seeing it as a burden, you can learn to view it as a part of your story, one that has shaped who you are today. Embracing this journey allows you to live fully, even as you carry the weight of the loss of your child with you.

A Blob with No Name

As time went on, I began to envision my grief not as a fleeting emotion or something intangible, but as a physical object – a dark grey blob with a sad face. Initially, it loomed over me, intimidating and overwhelming. I found myself fearful of its presence, and, at times, I confronted it with bursts of anger. But as the years rolled by, we transformed from strangers into uneasy acquaintances. Now, I've learnt to tolerate it.

This once-massive blob has diminished in size and now fits snugly in my pocket, and I hold the power over it when it makes an appearance. Interestingly, I've never given it a name or assigned it a gender; it simply exists in my world as a part of me. Because of this dynamic, I've managed to keep it at arm's length. It's amusing how this concept makes perfect sense to me, yet when I put it into words, I can't help but feel a bit like a mad scientist. Such is life!

A Nonlinear Journey Through a Complex Landscape

Grief becomes an integral part of who you are, influencing your thoughts, feelings, and experiences in ways you might not have anticipated. It shapes your perspective on life, relationships, and even the smallest moments of joy. Having a sense of control over 'it' really helped me regulate my emotions.

This journey isn't linear. There will be days filled with sunshine, where laughter comes easily and life feels comforting. There will also be dark days – oh, there will be many – leaving you gasping for breath. Both experiences are valid and natural. Accepting these fluctuations as part of your journey means you're allowing yourself the space to grieve while also making room for healing.

Your grief may manifest in unexpected ways – perhaps through memories that suddenly surface, an old song that brings tears to your eyes, or a place that holds special significance. These moments can floor you, but each one is an opportunity to acknowledge your feelings, to validate the depth of your love and loss. Allow yourself to feel these emotions fully.

As you navigate this complex landscape of grief, you might find that it guides you towards growth and resilience. In the midst of your sorrow, you may uncover strengths you didn't know you possessed. This transformation can lead to a deeper understanding of yourself and a renewed appreciation for life, even in its imperfections.

It's essential to remember that healing doesn't mean forgetting. Your child will always hold a place in your heart, and their memory will continue to influence your life.

Instead of trying to erase your grief, focus on integrating it into your life in a way that feels authentic. This might mean celebrating milestones, finding joy in new experiences while still carrying your memories close, or seeking connections with others who share your journey.

Ultimately, by acknowledging your grief and allowing yourself the space to feel and heal, you can find a way to live a meaningful and fulfilling life. Embracing this journey doesn't mean you have to sacrifice your pain; instead, it allows you to honour it while discovering new paths forward. Through this process, you may find that love, hope, and resilience can coexist alongside your grief, enriching your life in unexpected ways. Each step you take can be a testament to your strength and a celebration of the love that remains, reminding you that, even in the darkest moments, there is the possibility of light.

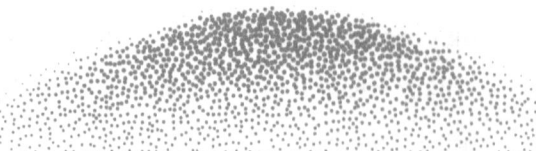

A Breath of Wisdom

Living with loss means finding a way to move forward while carrying your grief with you.

Grief can manifest in unexpected ways, each one providing an opportunity to acknowledge the depth of your love and loss.

Healing doesn't mean forgetting.

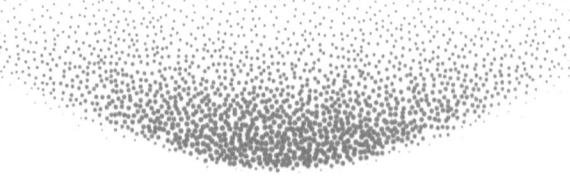

Resources for Grieving Parents

These resources offer a range of support options, from counselling to community connections, and can be incredibly helpful for grieving parents as they navigate their journey of loss. While some of these resources I have personally used, others I have not. Please approach them with care and consider your own needs when seeking assistance.

Support Groups and Helplines

COMPANY	SUPPORT OFFERED	CONTACT
Red Nose/ Sands Australia	Support for parents after the loss of a baby and support and resources for bereaved parents and safe sleeping for babies	sands.org.au rednosegriefandloss.org.au 24/7 bereavement support line: 1300 308 307 General enquiries: 1300 998 698 support@rednose.org.au
Stillbirth Foundation Australia	Resources and support for stillbirth	stillbirthfoundation.org.au 02 9557 9070 office@stillbirthfoundation.org.au
The Compassionate Friends Australia	Peer support for parents grieving the loss of a child	tcfa.org.au National grief line: 1300 064 068 State-based organisations – check website for details.
PANDA (Perinatal Anxiety & Depression Australia)	Support for families dealing with perinatal loss	panda.org.au Helpline (Monday to Saturday): 1300 726 306 quality@panda.org.au
Griefline	Telephone support for those experiencing grief	griefline.org.au Helpline (7 days): 1300 845 745

Support Groups and Helplines (continued)

Beyond Blue	Mental health support, including resources for grief	beyondblue.org.au Counselling services: 1300 224 636 beyondblue.org.au/get-support/talk-to-a-counsellor/email/Email-Support-Service-form
Lifeline	24/7 crisis support and suicide prevention	lifeline.org.au Chat 24/7: 13 11 14 Text 24/7: 0477 13 11 14
Kids Helpline	Counselling for young people aged 5 to 25	kidshelpline.com.au 1800 551 800
SuicideLine	24/7 telephone and online counselling service for those affected by suicide in Melbourne and Victoria	suicideline.org.au 1300 651 251
Suicide Call Back Service	A free nationwide service providing 24/7 phone and online counselling to people affected by suicide	suicidecallbackservice.org.au 1300 659 467

RESOURCES FOR GRIEVING PARENTS

Online Support and Forums

COMPANY	SUPPORT OFFERED	WEBSITE
Bittersweet Parents	Facebook group providing support for bereaved parents	facebook.com/groups/bittersweetparents (Approval required by admin to join)
GriefShare	Online grief support group and resources	griefshare.org
Beyond Blue Forums	Online community for those affected by grief	forums.beyondblue.org.au
Butterfly Foundation	Support for eating disorders, including those triggered by grief	butterfly.org.au

Local Support Services

COMPANY	SUPPORT OFFERED
Local hospitals and clinics	Many offer bereavement support services
Community health centres	Check for local bereavement programs

Professional Counselling Services

COMPANY	SUPPORT OFFERED	CONTACT	NOTES
Australian Psychological Society (APS)	Find a psychologist specialising in grief	psychology.org.au	
Grief Centre	Counselling and support for bereaved families	griefcentre.com.au 1300 270 479 aftercare@griefcentre.com.au	This is not a crisis support or emergency support service
Relationships Australia	Counselling services for individuals and families	relationships.org.au 1300 364 277	State-based contact advised
Mental Health Foundation of Australia	Resources for mental health and grief	mhfa.org.au 1300 643 287 admin@mhfa.org.au	Operations in every state and territory in Australia

Art and Creative Therapies

COMPANY	SUPPORT OFFERED	CONTACT
Grief Australia – Art Therapy	Webinar	grief.org.au/ga/ga/Detail/Item_Details.aspx?iProductCode=OP210726&Category=RECWEB

Educational Resources

COMPANY	SUPPORT OFFERED	WEBSITE
University of Western Australia – Grief Resources	Academic resources on grief and loss	uwa.edu.au/students/ support-services/ mental-health-and-wellbeing
Raising Children Network – Grief and Loss	Information on supporting grieving children	raisingchildren.net. au/school-age/ connecting-communicating/ death-grief/ when-someone-dies

Memorial and Commemorative Organisations

COMPANY	SUPPORT OFFERED	CONTACT
Heartfelt	Volunteer photographers providing memories for families after loss	heartfelt.org.au 1800 583 768 office@heartfelt.org.au
Keepsake Jewellery Australia	Memorial jewellery	keepsakejewellery.com.au

Special Interest Groups

COMPANY	SUPPORT OFFERED	CONTACT
Multiple Births Australia	Support for parents grieving the loss of one or more of their multiples	amba.org.au 1300 886 499 enquiries@amba.org.au

Memorial Projects

COMPANY	SUPPORT OFFERED	CONTACT
Rally for Rhys Foundation	Fundraising for bereaved families	rallyforrhys.com.au rallyforrhys@outlook.com
Angel Gowns Australia	Creating gowns for stillborn babies	angelgownsaustralia.org.au enquiry@angelgownsaustralia.org.au

Podcasts and Online Talks

COMPANY	SUPPORT OFFERED	WEBSITE
Griefcast – Cariad Lloyd	Podcast discussing grief and loss	cariadlloyd.com/griefcast
Good Mourning	Online talks and interviews discussing grief and loss	goodmourning.com.au

Youth and Child Resources

COMPANY	SUPPORT OFFERED	CONTACT DETAILS
Feel the Magic	A grief education and support service for bereaved children, teens, and families	feelthemagic.org.au 1300 602 465 admin@feelthemagic.org.au
Kids Helpline	Counselling for young people aged 5 to 25	kidshelpline.com.au 1800 551 800
Whitelion	Support services for young people and families	whitelion.asn.au 1300 669 600 info@kidsfirstaustralia.org.au
Playgroup Australia	Programs that include support for grieving families	playgroupaustralia.org.au

Holistic Approaches

COMPANY	SUPPORT OFFERED
Meditation and mindfulness groups	Various local options for grief support
Yoga for grief	Classes and workshops focused on healing through movement

Other Resources

COMPANY	SUPPORT OFFERED	CONTACT DETAILS
Healing Hearts	Connecting bereaved families	healinghearts.net.au finn@healinghearts.net.au
Grief.com	International resources for those dealing with grief	grief.com
Wellbeing Australia	Resources for emotional wellbeing	wellbeingaustralia.com.au admin@wellbeingaustralia.com.au

Awareness Campaigns

Baby Loss Awareness Week (9–15 October)
International Pregnancy and Infant Loss Remembrance Day (15 October)
Worldwide Candle Lighting Day (second Sunday in December)
Bereaved Father's Day (last Sunday in August)
Bereaved Mother's Day (first Sunday in May)
International Bereaved Sibling Awareness Month (November)

Acknowledgements

Supporting bereaved parents on their journey can be overwhelming, but so many incredible people have walked this path alongside us. To all of you who have believed in me, even when the way forward was unclear, thank you from the bottom of my heart.

The entire team at Dean Publishing for embracing me and our story and working your magic to bring this book to life!

Mick, Julie, and our Blackbelt family – this book would not exist without your guidance, wisdom, mentorship, gentle encouragement, and unwavering inspiration.

Louise Kearns (PPP) – you keep me grounded and accountable, and I treasure that we share our journeys together.

To our dearest friends who have stood by us through every challenge, your support has lightened our hearts. For the thoughtful gestures, the texts just to check in, for remembering the important dates, and the late-night chats – we love you all deeply.

Joe and our DJH Team – you are like family to us, and we are profoundly grateful for each and every one of you.

To our parents, siblings, and extended family – we know you carry your own pain and grief, yet you continue to surround us with love and strength. We are so fortunate to have such a solid and caring family foundation.

To our beautiful children, Amalie and Elijah – you teach us so much every single day about bravery, resilience, love, and embracing life's risks. My wish for both of you is that you live lives full of wonder, always knowing that you are safe and loved beyond measure.

And finally, to our angel Rhys – we miss you every day. You guide us with your light, and your spirit will forever inspire us to push boundaries and give our all to everything we do. We choose to live in your honour, because you were denied that privilege. Mummy will teach others how to live beyond the pain of child loss. You are a truly special boy, Rhys. We love you endlessly.

About the Author

Shannon Hodgetts is a compassionate and dedicated published author, driven by a strong personal mission. Having endured the profound and heartbreaking loss of her child Rhys, she is determined to support and guide other parents navigating similar paths of grief. This deeply personal experience has instilled in Shannon a sense of urgency to connect with newly bereaved parents, offering them comfort, understanding, and companionship during their most challenging times.

Drawing from her own journey through grief, Shannon aims to share not only her story but also the insights and knowledge she has gained along the way. She recognises that each parent's experience is unique, yet there are universal emotions and challenges that bind them together. By articulating her thoughts and feelings through her writing, she hopes to create a safe space where parents can feel seen, heard, and validated in their grief. Her words serve as a lifeline, offering reassurance that they are not alone in their journey.

Beyond her writing endeavours, Shannon is passionate about reducing the stigma surrounding child loss – a topic that is often shrouded in silence and misunderstanding. She believes that open dialogue is essential for healing and wants to encourage others to share their stories without fear of judgement.

By shedding light on this often-overlooked aspect of parenthood, Shannon seeks to foster a greater sense of community and support among those who have experienced similar losses. Through her unwavering commitment, she is making a meaningful impact within the bereavement community. Her advocacy not only provides solace and support to those enduring the unimaginable but also helps to transform the narrative around grief, encouraging more parents to embrace their feelings and seek connection. Shannon's mission is a testament to the resilience of the human spirit and the profound healing that can come from sharing one's journey with others.

Audiobook

One Breath at a Time is also available in audio format.

Jump onto your favourite audiobook platform to have the story narrated for you by the author.

www.ingramcontent.com/pod-product-compliance
Lightning Source LLC
Chambersburg PA
CBHW022045290426
44109CB00014B/989